Recordkeeping Cultures

T0323455

Recordkeeping Cultures

Second edition

Gillian Oliver and **Fiorella Foscarini**

facet
publishing

Published by Facet Publishing
7 Ridgmount Street, London WC1E 7AE
www.facetpublishing.co.uk

Facet Publishing is wholly owned by CILIP: the Library and Information Association.

British Library Cataloguing in Publication Data
A catalogue record for this book is available from the British Library.

ISBN 978-1-78330-399-1 (paperback)
ISBN 978-1-78330-400-4 (hardback)
ISBN 978-1-78330-401-1 (e-book)

First published 2020

Text printed on FSC accredited material.

Typeset from authors' files in 10/14 pt Palatino Linotype and Frutiger by Flagholme Publishing Services.
Printed and made in Great Britain by CPI Group (UK) Ltd, Croydon, CR0 4YY.

Contents

Figures and tables

Figures

Tables

Introduction to the second edition

The twofold purpose of the first edition of this book, *Records Management and Information Culture: Tackling the people problem*, holds true for this second edition. Firstly, the motivation to do something about the messy and difficult issues which are inevitable when we attempt to manage records in organisations and communities. Why are they inevitable? Because organisations are made up of people, who have different backgrounds, goals and expectations, and whose primary purpose as employees is to perform work as set out in their position descriptions. Each individual will have some responsibilities related to the creation and management of records and information, but in the majority of cases, such responsibilities will not be itemised in their job descriptions. The magnitude of this people problem has been frequently described anecdotally but now there is empirical evidence available in the outcomes of the University of Northumbria's research project into electronic records management issues. The headline findings from this global project included the following:

> Participants identified people issues as part of all three facets investigated [i.e. people, processes and technology]. They are predominant, fundamental and challenging because they concern culture, philosophical attitudes, awareness of records management and ERM [electronic records management] issues, preferences, knowledge and skills.
>
> (McLeod et al., 2011, 73–4)

A further finding from the same project was particularly striking, as it points to some critical features in the way that we work that may in fact prove to be detrimental to achieving our goals:

Records professionals were open enough to recognise they may be part of the problem as well as part of the solution. On the positive side, records professionals take a holistic view and have the principles and tools to manage records; however their demands may be unrealistic or too constraining. Respondents identified a range of attitudes of records managers and their approaches to ERM that should be avoided …

(McLeod et al., 2011, 79–80)

These findings have been echoed in subsequent studies, for example in Sir Alex Allan's review of electronic recordkeeping in British government departments. Summary findings included the following comments:

Existing systems which require individual users to identify documents that should constitute official records, and then to save them into an EDRMS [electronic document and records management system] or corporate file plan, have not worked well. The processes have been burdensome and compliance poor. As a result, almost all departments have a mass of digital data stored on shared drives that is poorly organised and indexed.

and

Even with improved systems, there will be a need to ensure the appropriate culture is embedded in departments and that changes are backed up by a high level push to make sure new procedures are followed in practice.

(Allan, 2014)
https://www.gov.uk/government/publications/
government-digital-records-and-archives-review-by-sir-alex-allan

Secondly, the specific objective of this book is to demonstrate a way in which progress can be made towards addressing the issues identified above. This second edition extends the discussion of information culture presented in the first edition, modifying the Information Culture Framework (ICF) to facilitate its application to recordkeeping environments, so as to assist in developing sound recordkeeping cultures.

The research that we undertook in our subsequent academic roles is summarised in Chapter 1, as these findings are directly relevant to the approach taken to information culture assessment throughout the book. The second edition is informed by the outcomes of further case studies conducted between 2015 and 2017, together with feedback from workshops and presentations conducted around the world. We are especially grateful to the International Council on Archives (ICA) for supporting much of this work, which has resulted in the development of a toolkit to assess information cultures, and an online community of practice.

This book consolidates ideas relating to what the concept of information culture involves, why it is important, and how it can be applied to actual recordkeeping situations, including both how to carry out analysis of a given organisation and what to do with your findings.

The audience for this book is primarily practitioners, but also individuals working in academic contexts. Practitioners will include all those with responsibilities for creating and maintaining processes to ensure that authentic, reliable, usable records with integrity are captured into organisational systems. The core of this group will undoubtedly be records managers and archivists, but it is to be hoped that other individuals rapidly becoming involved with the challenges of managing information as evidence for accountability purposes (such as information technology (IT) specialists), will also be able to draw on this book as a resource.

The academic audience will include those both teaching and researching in the areas of records management and archives, but also in related fields, such as information systems, knowledge management and information management. It is envisaged that this book will provide material for the development of education and training programmes focusing on how to implement recordkeeping systems in organisations, how to communicate recordkeeping goals and how to understand the environment you are working in. We also hope it will stimulate further ideas for research into information culture, which, we are convinced, has very real value for the successful management of information not only in organisations but also at a national or societal level.

The book is divided into seven parts. The first of these consists of a single chapter, which provides the background for what follows. This preliminary chapter establishes the overall context, with a literature review of information culture, reporting on research to date. It explains the relevance of information culture to the 21st-century workplace, and spells out why recordkeeping cultures in particular deserve special attention within the current information landscape. The chapter also introduces the Information Culture Framework (ICF) – a three-level pyramid where the factors that influence attitudes and values towards information in organisations are identified and ranked according to their susceptibility to change – which has been further developed in this second edition.

Parts 2, 3, 4 and 5 each address aspects of the framework, beginning in Part

2 with level one, Fundamental influences. This part considers those factors which may appear difficult if not impossible to change – but which are essential to identify and to be taken into account if appropriate interventions are to be developed. Each of the three chapters included in this part considers one set of influences, namely the value accorded to records, information preferences, and language and national (or regional) technological infrastructure. Although the factors considered at this level are hard to change, knowing what they are is invaluable in terms of guiding records management programme development. What comes first? How can uptake be promoted? What types of leadership are required? All these questions and more are answered.

Part 3 (comprising Chapters 5 and 6) considers the knowledge, skills and expertise of staff members relating to records, from the perspectives of recordkeeping and digital literacy; and also their awareness of relevant legislative, legal and other mandatory requirements. These cultural influences belong to the second level of the ICF, that is, an intermediate level comprising factors that organisational actors can improve by taking specific measures. Thus, Part 3 provides guidance on identifying training needs, and on developing appropriate training programmes. Suggestions for developing context-appropriate training (when it is best to use online resources, group versus one-to-one sessions, etc.) are provided.

Part 4 consists of a single chapter (Chapter 7), and addresses the topmost level of the ICF, the characteristics that are unique to a particular organisation and thus probably the most amenable to change. This layer level has been modified in this edition for a more specific focus on recordkeeping environments. The first characteristic is corporate information governance, including information technology architecture. The second relates to recordkeeping systems and tools, for example, EDRMS, classification systems, retention plans. This final layer level can be the most productive area for action, and the discussion focuses on techniques for working collaboratively with IT colleagues as well as how to adopt a critically reflective perspective on current records management systems, policies and processes.

Part 5 of the book (consisting of Chapter 8) considers influences on all three levels of the ICF pyramid. These metalevels refer to two broad factors, namely trust in recordkeeping systems and records professionals, and language and communication. Both trust and language were included within the pyramid as outlined in the first edition, and assigned to specific levels (trust at level three and language at level one). Our experience leading up to this second edition has indicated that these factors are more diffuse, hence their new positioning as metalevels.

Part 6 (Chapter 9) introduces totally new content, namely the diagnostic factors identified in the course of developing a toolkit for the ICA. The factors are genres, workarounds and infrastructure, and we provide a number of examples from practice.

Part 7 brings everything together, starting with discussion of education in Chapter 10: how to teach information culture concepts and methods in archives and records programmes and training courses. Chapter 10 concludes by presenting an overall view of the assessment of information culture and subsequent actions.

References

Allan, Sir Alex (2014). Government Digital Records and Archives Review., https://www.gov.uk/government/publications/government-digital-records-and-archives-review-by-sir-alex-allan

McLeod, J., Childs, S. and Hardiman, R. (2011). Accelerating Positive Change in Electronic Records Management – Headline Findings from a Major Research Project, *Archives and Manuscripts*, **39** (2), 66–94.

PART 1

CHAPTER 1

Background and context

Every organisation, society, or community, has an information culture, or even multiple information cultures. Being able to analyse and understand these cultures is instrumental in developing records management programmes and systems that take people – the employees of the organisation, the members of the society or community – into account. The purpose of this initial chapter is to provide the background detail which describes and explains the foundations of the assessment framework discussed in the subsequent chapters.

This chapter begins by tracking the origins of the concept of information culture, and explaining why recordkeeping cultures deserve special attention, despite the current 'convergence' trends that tend to prioritise the notion of information over data and records (Yeo, 2018). Reporting on efforts to date studying information culture from societal, national and organisational perspectives, the latter perspective is emphasised because of its key relevance to records management in the 21st-century workplace. At this organisational level, two incompatible (alternative) points of view can be identified: one that regards an information culture as being conducive to good information management, and the other that takes the view that all organisations have an information culture, no matter how effective the latter may be perceived to be.

This then leads into the specific theoretical orientation influencing our approach to information culture, which is the records continuum. We explain how information culture is an integral part of a new conceptualisation of records management: recordkeeping informatics. This chapter then provides an overall introduction to the Information Culture Framework (ICF), briefly explaining the different levels, of the Framework and the relationships between them.

Finally, the ICF is clearly differentiated by considering it in the context of other evaluation methodologies and tools, such as information audits, information maturity, DIRKS (State Records New South Wales' Design and Implementation of Recordkeeping Systems), the Impact Calculator, and ARMA (Association of Records Managers and Administrators) International's Generally Accepted Recordkeeping Principles (GARP).

The concepts of information culture and recordkeeping culture

Information culture has been studied from two main perspectives: societal (including national) and organisational. The main focus of this book is on organisational information culture, a concept that we redefine more appropriately as recordkeeping culture; but societal- and national-level considerations have to be acknowledged, as these different approaches are not by any means mutually exclusive. Anyone concerned with organisational information culture or recordkeeping culture cannot fail to be concerned with discussions occurring at the other levels, as these will influence and provide insight into what happens in workplaces and communities. So, before introducing the ideas specifically relating to organisational information culture we will briefly sketch out some of the thinking around societal- and national-level views.

Societal information culture

Analysing information culture from a societal level necessitates a much broader and more philosophical view of the changes inherent in our information environment than at the organisational level, that which is the main focus of this book. Societal information culture can be understood as encompassing the influences on, and interactions between, human cultural expression and information systems of all types, including both technological and legal systems. Looking at information culture in this big-picture way considers the rapidly changing and expanding power of information considered in the context of new and emerging technologies that enable developments in our everyday lives, such as social media and mobile banking. Taking this societal perspective may provide a predictive, explanatory frame of reference to help us start to grapple with the complexities of the digital age.

But what is 'information'? And how can the pervasive nature of information be studied in a meaningful way? Luke Tredinnick, for example, takes a holistic view in attempting to describe our current information environment as a digital information culture (Tredinnick, 2008). The focus of his work is the influence of new information technologies on our everyday life, from the perspective that these new technologies have a transformational effect. He approaches digital information culture by singling out the following issues for discussion: textuality, authenticity, knowledge, power, identity and memory. He places his work in the context of ongoing attempts to make sense of the changing nature of communication and role of information technologies, such as Marshall McLuhan's *Understanding Media: the Extensions of Man* (1964) and Alvin Toffler's *Future Shock* (1970). In so doing, Tredinnick emphasises throughout the ongoing nature of such change, concluding with the words: 'The last chapter of socio-cultural change always remains unwritten' (p. 168).

However, by taking such a holistic approach, we might however lose sight of the specific meanings and practices that disciplines like archival studies and records management have developed over the centuries to make sure that records, as 'the foundation of social life and activity' (Yeo, 2018, 151), are created and managed properly. This is one of the main arguments put forward by Geoffrey Yeo in his latest book (2018), where the role of records as persistent evidence and reliable memory of our actions is discussed. We all live in an 'information society' and collaboration among experts in the various information-related fields is absolutely necessary. Nevertheless, Yeo reminds us that 'perspectives of the different disciplines should be treated with appropriate respect' (p. 193).

Memory and forgetting

The concept of memory in any information culture perspective is an important one – even more so within a recordkeeping context. As records managers we are concerned with organisational memory, which will be influenced by technological developments in society. Viktor Mayer-Schönberger (2009) focuses on one particular aspect of memory that is changing rapidly. That is, the power to forget, and the danger of losing that ability to forget in a time when information is stored in vast virtual warehouses, and commercial interest drivers provide motivators for continued 'remembering' even when existing norms would seem to dictate the opposite. Mayer-Schönberger explores remembering and forgetting through history, charting the development of tools to assist in remembering, from pictures through the development of script to print, all striving towards an ideal of perfect recall.

The author paints a rich picture of the usages of technology enabling the creation of a perfect digital memory. Usages of technology range from our active participation in constructing virtual lives in social networking sites such as Facebook, to our unwitting involvement in surveillance activities, such as Google and Microsoft collecting data showing our online presence, reflecting our interests, thoughts and dreams. This perfect memory may be more comprehensive than we ever thought possible, but forgetting, an essential component of memory, has shifted from being the default position to not being there unless it is consciously specified.

Mayer-Schönberger emphasises that although technology provides the power to construct this 'perfect' and comprehensive digital memory, it rests with humans to change the situation. Possible solutions proposed and trialled include the following. Firstly, digital abstinence, in other words individuals taking responsibility for their digital footprint, and increased awareness so that people will exercise more judgement in what information they share publicly. This is a topic that is further discussed in Chapter 5. Another set of strategies rests on information privacy legislation and regulation, and the construction of an infrastructure for digital privacy rights. The author also proposes a further suggestion, that is, to assign an expiration date to information, and presents this as a novel answer to a new situation. A combination of these approaches is undoubtedly required, but the suggestion of an expiration date should particularly resonate with records managers. For anyone well versed in the principles of records management this is of course very familiar and well-known territory – assigning retention periods to information, instituting systematic review and destruction or transferring to archival custody are the very essence of recordkeeping practice.

As mentioned earlier, it is important to recognise that recordkeeping has its specific place within the broader information field. However, this should not suggest that records experts have to clearly demarcate their areas of responsibility (this is a record, this isn't …), although some of them may be tempted to do so as a way to cope with what can seem an impossible workload. By circumscribing their domain and operating selectively rather than inclusively, records managers and archivists will become more and more marginalised and risk appearing increasingly irrelevant. It is their specialised knowledge that should guide their actions, not the 'inherent' qualities of the materials under their purview. Their expertise with the nuances of forgetting, the robust policies and procedures that they have developed to ensure short-term and long-term memories, their awareness of the need to strike a balance between the right to know and the protection of privacy, have the potential to contribute greatly to the debate about perfect digital memories which is now occurring at the societal level. The complex set of strategies identified by Mayer-Schönberger to make sure forgetting is a component in our societal digital memory should inspire records managers to extend the reach of their procedures and be open to suggestions coming from other disciplinary areas.

Social media, truth and fake news

Concerns about social media have been discussed for a number of years now, culminating in reports of the use of social media channels to influence the outcome of democratic processes. One of the first high-profile commentaries was Andrew Keen's *The Cult of the Amateur* (2007), highlighting the downside of new, enabling technologies. His view of the effect that information technology (IT), in the form of the internet, is having on our minds, on our very ability to think and reason, is a very negative one. The subtitle of this book is *How today's internet is killing our culture and assaulting our economy*, which sends a very clear signal about the author's view of digital technologies. He equates today's technology-enabled world with T. H. Huxley's infinite monkey theory: if an infinite number of monkeys are provided with an infinite number of typewriters, the chances are that some monkey will produce a masterpiece (Keen, 2007, 2). He then proceeds to extend the analogy, first to blogs:

> At the heart of the infinite monkey experiment in self publishing is the Internet diary, the ubiquitous blog. Blogging has become such a mania that a new blog is being created every second of every minute of every hour of every day. We are blogging with monkeylike shamelessness about our private lives, our sex lives, our dream lives, our lack of lives, our Second Lives.
>
> (Keen, 2007, 3)

and then to YouTube videos:

> YouTube eclipses even the blogs in the inanity and absurdity of its content. Nothing seems too prosaic or narcissistic for these videographer monkeys. The site is an infinite gallery of amateur movies showing poor fools dancing, singing, eating, washing, shopping, driving, cleaning, sleeping, or just staring into their computers.
>
> (Keen, 2007, 5)

These are provocative views, which some will find deeply disturbing, but which will strike a harmonious chord in others. Regardless of readers' reactions, what does become clear is the need for change. The sheer scale and variety of types of information, coupled with the changing roles of authorship and publication, need vastly different sets of skills on the part of both information creators and consumers in order to make sense of this new world of technology-enhanced information. Chapter 5 will further explore the dimensions of digital literacy.

The relevance of the web world of social media, including tweets, blogs and YouTube videos, to recordkeepers cannot be understated. We are concerned with authenticity, with information that is characterised by integrity and reliability. An age where 'fake news' is used as a rallying cry provides an opportunity for engagement, to demonstrate professional knowledge and competencies, more than ever before. On a more practical level, as more and more organisations and communities in both the private and public sectors use social media as communications tools, records managers need to develop the appropriate strategies to manage this information as evidence for accountability purposes. To be effective, these strategies have to fit with the culture of the organisation and to seamlessly integrate with the way that people work, rather than hinder or obstruct workflows. Diagnosing the organisation's information and recordkeeping cultures is the essential first step to achieving these objectives, and this is only possible if we have a good understanding of these societal perspectives.

The work of Tredinnick, Mayer-Schönberger and Keen is cited here to give examples of the emergence of concerns about society's information culture. Subsequent events such as the Brexit referendum and the US election in 2016 show that the issues and challenges that our information age poses are increasing in complexity, and societal information culture will continue to attract attention from researchers and commentators. This is the overall context in which we work at organisational level; all is part of the discourse that frames and influences our attempts at records management.

Discussion of societal information culture is usually presented as being universally applicable, although some may dispute this on the basis that the environment under scrutiny is primarily that of the Western, developed world. Tredinnick's discussion of the development of written language and printing, for instance, is Eurocentric (2008, 59–76); Mayer-Schönberger does not take indigenous views into account when considering attitudes towards sharing of information and knowledge (2009, 131–4); Keen equates widespread access to broadband in the USA as an indicator of a fully connected, networked society (2007, 15). Despite this, it is possible to distinguish considerations of information culture that clearly have a more explicit focus on particular countries.

Focusing on a specific country

Various researchers have applied the information culture lens to specific national settings, for example China (Zheng, 2005), the Maldives (Riyaz and Smith, 2012) and Hungary (Szecskö, 1986). In addition, there are of course many other studies that have been conducted on various features or dimensions of information culture (for example, information policy in Canada [Nilsen, 1994], Brazil [Rosenberg, 1982] or Norway [Audunson and Nordlie, 2003]) but it is beyond the scope of this book to provide a comprehensive analysis of this literature. However, when attempting to analyse the information culture of a particular country, the first step would be to search for relevant literature on specific features such as information literacy, information technology, legislation, and so on. Our organisational-level perspective necessarily takes into account the legislative, linguistic and technological features associated with the country that the organisation is situated in. These features, which often have a supranational character (e.g. the European Union [EU] legislation, most languages spoken in the world, and the internet are all phenomena that cross national boundaries), are discussed in the context of the ICF in Chapters 4 and 8.

Information culture in organisations

Ideas about cultural influences on the ways in which information is managed, accessed and used in organisations have been discussed and explored since the 1980s (see, for instance, Brown and Starkey, 1994; Curry and Moore, 2003; Davenport, Eccles, and Prusak, 1992; Davenport and Prusak, 1997; Jarvenpaa and Staples, 2000, 2001). Understandings and interpretations, though, vary greatly. The first mention of information culture specifically is generally credited to Mariam Ginman, who used the phrase to characterise a particular organisational type, namely one with a management style responsive to information from the external environment and open to change and innovation (Ginman, 1993). This research resulted in some considerable interest from the special library community, and led to a proposal presented to the British Library to investigate the correlation between information culture and successful business performance (Grimshaw, 1995). Information culture has been specifically linked to recognition of the critical nature of information in organisations, so and is defined as a setting conducive to effective information management:

> The value and utility of information in achieving operational and strategic goals is recognised, where information forms the basis of organizational decision-making and Information Technology is readily exploited as an enabler for effective Information Systems.
>
> (Curry and Moore, 2003)

This body of work seems to focus on a 'culture of information' perspective. Following on from this, attention has turned to investigating the ways in which people interact with and use information in organisations.

In Europe, research has been undertaken to explore the relationship between information culture and information behaviours in organisations, notably led by Gunilla Widén-Wulff (Widén-Wulff, 2000; Widén-Wulff et al., 2008; Widén-Wulff and Ginman, 2004; Widén and Hansen, 2012; Widén and Karim, 2018).

In Canada, studies of the relationship between information culture and information use have been carried out. A survey of three Canadian organisations concluded that information culture significantly affects information use outcomes. Information use outcomes are defined as including the shaping of new knowledge, contributing to decision-making and influencing and exchanging information with colleagues (Choo et al., 2008, 796). This research formulated definitions of information behaviours and values, based on Marchand et al. (2002). The variables identified were as shown in Table 1.1.

Table 1.1 *Information behaviours and values* (from Choo et al., 2008, 796)

Research variable	Definition
Information sharing	Willingness to provide others with information in an appropriate and collaborative manner
Information proactivity	Active concern to obtain and apply new information to respond to changes and to promote innovation
Information transparency	Openness in reporting information on errors and failures, thus allowing learning from mistakes
Information integrity	Use of information in a trustful and principled manner at the individual and organisational level
Information informality	Willingness to use and trust informal sources over institutionalised information
Information control	Presenting information to people to manage and monitor their performance

The definitions provided for these variables indicate that they can only provide only a partial reflection of the information culture of an organisation. They do not encompass the broader view of organisational and environmental systems which influence information governance. Similarly, no distinction is made between information as a source of knowledge and information as evidence; accountability is not mentioned. However, the variables do include those that seem to be related to trust (especially information integrity and information informality).

Janine Douglas studied the information culture of state government departments in Australia, resulting in a proposed new definition of information culture:

> An information culture is an emerging complex system of values, attitudes,
> beliefs and behaviours that influence how information is used in an
> organisation. It exists in the context of, and is influenced by, an organisational
> culture and wider environments.
>
> (Douglas, 2010, 307)

Again, there is a clear emphasis on information *use,* which does not seem to acknowledge the ongoing *creation* of information within organisations, nor its *maintenance* when it may not be frequently used. Importantly, however, the definition does recognise the influence of organisational culture and external factors. The general philosophy underlying this approach still seems to lie in the 'culture of information' camp.

Another exploration of information culture (Martin et al., 2003) distinguished information *cultures* (plural) as differentiating between the business and the information technology function in an organisation. These authors' depiction of an effectively functioning information-intensive organisation is one where the information culture is integrated, i.e. where similar values and attitudes to information are present across the board. These findings are useful in that they acknowledge the likely existence of subcultures within an organisation, and do not assume a pre-existing uniform set of beliefs and values.

Our organisational research

Our interest in information and recordkeeping cultures has been fuelled by research studies undertaken independently, but which highlighted a shared concern for developing a much more nuanced understanding of organisational contexts than has previously existed. Gillian undertook three case studies which looked at ways in which organisations carrying out the same functions in regions of the world that are likely to have very different cultural profiles manage information (see Oliver, [2008] for overall findings from this project).

Gillian found that there were clearly very distinct differences in the ways in which individuals in these three organisations approached the creation and management of the information needed to record business activities. More discussion of the possible influence of national cultural dimensions on information management can be found in her work on organisational culture (Oliver, 2011). Not surprisingly, many of those features are relevant to the current consideration of records management and the ICF in this book, so more detail about cultural dimensions can be found in Chapter 3.

However, although a key area of interest of Gillian's was to discover linkages between values and behaviours towards information and national cultural differences, it was clearly apparent that the situation was more complex than could be explained by restricting consideration to national cultural dimensions. An additional case study looked at the work carried out by the committee responsible for drafting the international standard on records management, ISO15489. The content was based on a pre-existing document, the Australian standard on records management, and thus it should not have taken a great deal of time and effort to reshape this for an international audience. The fact that it did take a number of years has been attributed to the differing national factions represented on the negotiating committee. However, on talking to those involved Gillian discovered that occupational differences – conflicting viewpoints put forward by records managers and archivists – appeared to be the primary reason for the long, drawn-out process (Oliver, 2011, 104–6). A follow-up study drew attention for the important role of social capital, as a means of navigating clashes of culture and achieving consensus (Oliver, 2014).

Inspired by Gillian's study on the relationship between recordkeeping practices and national cultural differences, Fiorella drew on some of Hofstede's (2001) ideas in her doctoral dissertation research (Foscarini, 2009). Sociologist Geert Hofstede developed a matrix in which two cultural dimensions – that, in his view, would be crucial to define the character of any organised group (i.e. power distance and uncertainty avoidance) – are matched against types of bureaucracies (from full bureaucracy to the village market) and geographic regions. Despite Hofstede's deterministic approach, his matrix appeared to be a useful framework to identify a number of institutions (national central banks, in the case of Fiorella's study) located in different countries, each likely to be associated with a specific organisational configuration. The purpose of this case-study research was to investigate how people understand and use the notion of business function when dealing with function-based records classification systems, either as developers or as users of such systems. Findings confirmed that some types of organisations (namely, traditional, full bureaucracies) are more conducive than others to the straightforward application of the functional approach.

More importantly, through her study Fiorella started to identify 'factors' that appeared to affect people's perceptions of their responsibilities towards the corporate record, their willingness to accept a new (functional) system, their ways of making sense of the new system (also known as 'appropriation moves' [DeSanctis and Poole, 1994]), and so on. Such factors had to do with the employees' professional backgrounds, the adoption of certain management philosophies at higher levels in the organisation, political motives, and internal group dynamics. This analysis made her conclude that a 'redefinition of the analytical skills that records professionals should be equipped with' (Foscarini, 2012, 32) would seem to be necessary. This book aims at providing its readers with the 'soft' skills that will help them to unveil the deep motives underlying organisational processes and behaviours, and take appropriate actions.

The above research findings led to a definition of information culture as **the values accorded to information, and attitudes towards it, specifically within organisational contexts**. Thus two views of organisational information culture emerge from the literature, reminiscent of the different use of the term applied in national studies. One perspective considers 'cultures of information' where the concept is used to describe environments which are conducive to the management of information. The other acknowledges the universal nature of information culture, regardless of whether effective usage or management of information is a characteristic.

The approach taken in this book is unequivocally in the second category, and the focus of this second edition is specifically on recordkeeping environments. As emphasised in the previous edition, all organisations have an information culture, no matter what sector they are active in, where in the world they are located, regardless of their size, complexity and the extent of their information technology capabilities. From a recordkeeping perspective, communities must be added to the picture, as these oftentimes independent and less formal types of social aggregations may display recordkeeping-culture characteristics that could be taken as a model by mainstream institutions. As our study of organisational and information cultures has demonstrated, some elements of information culture are more amenable to change than others. The framework for assessment, which is described later in this chapter, makes clear distinctions between these constituent elements. But first it is necessary to provide the theoretical background for this approach: continuum theory.

Underlying theory

Most recordkeeping professionals (records managers and archivists) will have heard of Frank Upward's records continuum theory. Much less well known, however, are the related continua models that have subsequently been developed to apply the same thinking to other specialist areas, such as cultural heritage, information systems and publishing (Upward, 2000), so it is useful to delve beyond the familiar dimensional representation of the records continuum. In this book, both the information continuum and records continuum are drawn on, and so they are briefly discussed below.

The basis of continuum theory is Anthony Giddens' structuration theory (Upward, 1997). The essence of structuration theory is the recognition of the duality of agency and structure: one affects the other, recursively. To grossly over-simplify, nothing stays the same, society is in a constant state of flux, as organisations change in response to their environment so their environment changes, and thus the organisation will again adapt to those new conditions – and so on and so on. This theoretical setting facilitates the recognition of the fluid, slippery nature of information, the ongoing development of new technologies as well as the structural environment shaped by legislation and standards.

The information continuum

The information continuum was originally developed as a teaching tool by academics (Don Schauder, Barbara Reed and Frank Upward) at the School of Information Management at Monash University in Melbourne, Australia. The school's master's degree programme was a holistic one, encompassing professional education for both librarians and recordkeepers, and it was necessary to clearly articulate the different needs of these professional groups. At the heart of the information continuum model is the recognition of the different *purposes* for which library and recordkeeping professionals manage information. Librarians manage information primarily for the purpose of promoting knowledge or awareness, and also in some settings (the public library domain, for instance) for the purpose of entertainment. Records managers and archivists, however, primarily manage information as evidence, for the purpose of accountability. These primary purposes do not negate the existence of other, secondary purposes, but serve to establish some primary settings for the uses of different techniques and application of different policies.

This distinction of unique purpose for records managers and archivists is a critical consideration, and is of immense benefit in considering the comprehensiveness and utility of other information culture definitions and models. There is virtually no acknowledgement from other information culture researchers of the need to consider information as evidence; emphasis on information-seeking behaviour and information use does not highlight accountability needs.

The records continuum

The records continuum (Figure 1.1) provides a way of making sense of the complexity of recordkeeping in our digital environment. The four dimensions (create, capture, organise and pluralise) and the four axes (recordkeeping, evidential, transactional and identity) can be used as a practical tool to identify at which stage of development an organisation is at in terms of managing its information as evidence, for accountability.

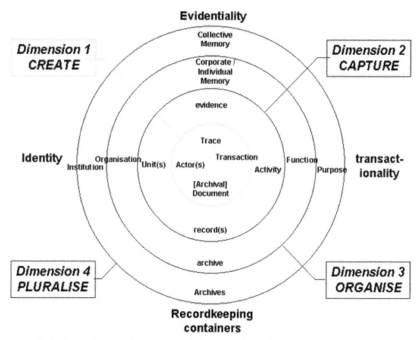

Figure 1.1 *Records continuum model, reproduced with permission of Frank Upward*

The first dimension, create, is where all individual employees are actively creating information to perform their business. Second-dimension (capture) activities occur if sufficient controls (e.g. assigning relevant metadata such as a meaningful file name, storing the information in a location that can be accessed by multiple individuals, such as a shared directory or filing cabinet) are applied that enable the information to be accessed by other individuals within the same team or workgroup. It is only in the third dimension, organise, where it can be considered that the controls that will ensure the maintenance of the critical characteristics of records (usability, authenticity, integrity and reliability) are applied and, depending on access requirements, information is made available across the organisation. The fourth dimension, pluralise, refers to the deployment of information outside the creating and maintaining organisation, in response to broader societal needs.

For the purposes of this book, and the aim of analysing information culture with a view to developing a culture conducive to records management, it is important to understand that these ideas are developed in the context of continuum theory. The perceived inadequacy of current records management practice to achieve the goal of successfully comprehensively managing information for accountability in organisations has led to a proposal for a new disciplinary approach to this area: recordkeeping informatics.

Recordkeeping informatics

The absence of a current records management textbook that truly reflected continuum thinking was the primary motivator for one of us (Gillian) to collaborate with Barbara Reed, Frank Upward and Joanne Evans to develop ideas for a totally new approach to records management (Upward et al., 2013). Two fundamental ideas that underpinned their thinking were as follows:

1 The problematic assumption that records can be managed. This implies that records are fixed and unchanging; once identified (by, for instance, a records management survey) these are assets that can be controlled by imposing means. This does not reflect the nature of today's workplace, characterised by multiple formal and informal information channels, systems and processes, where every employee is likely to be creating and (re-)using records whether they are aware of it or not. The inherent fluidity of most systems used to create and manage today's records (e.g. web-based interactive systems, dynamic databases) contributes to their instability.
2 Records managers are not the only key players involved in managing organisational information, particularly where the transactions of an organisation's activities are recorded in multiple business systems (for instance, human resources and finance systems, enterprise information management systems, and so on). There is a need for all information professionals to be able to work together collaboratively, each bringing their own particular expertise to the mix. The situation could be viewed

as analogous to health care, where the role of general practitioner is widely understood as providing primary care, and specialists (neurologists, paediatricians, dermatologists, etc.) are referred to as and when necessary. It is perhaps a sign of insecurity that records managers seek to defend their turf against information technology incomers and that the environment seems to be more competitive than collaborative.

The juxtaposition of these two ideas seemed to depict records managers in a King Canute-type role, unable to effectively control the ever-increasing tide of information recording organisational transactions, and inevitably lacking the broad range of technical skills and expertise necessary to manage all organisational systems. The end result, of course, would be records managers becoming an extinct species. This situation cannot be addressed by simply re-branding and claiming a more inclusive (but even more unclear) title of information manager, but needs a paradigmatic shift in thinking, and understanding the nature of the ways in which information as evidence needs to be managed in order to provide accountability of actions.

This thinking led to the reconceptualisation of records management as *recordkeeping informatics*.

Informatics has been defined as follows:

Informatics is the science of information. It studies the representation, processing, and communication of information in natural and artificial systems. Since computers, individuals and organizations all process information, informatics has computational, cognitive and social aspects. Used as a compound, in conjunction with the name of a discipline, as in medical informatics, bio-informatics, etc., it denotes the specialization of informatics to the management and processing of data, information and knowledge in the named discipline.

(Fourman, 2003)

In this case, the 'named discipline' is recordkeeping. Combining these two concepts signifies the specialist nature of the focus of concern for records managers, and at the same time acknowledges that there are technological, cognitive and social aspects that have to be taken into account. The essential nature of information culture is signalled by its inclusion as one of the three facets for analysis in *Recordkeeping Informatics* (Upward et al., 2018). It is of prime importance to understand the environment in which practice is occurring in order to develop and apply successful interventions.

The information culture assessment framework

The case studies that were carried out in Germany, Australia and Hong Kong enabled Gillian to describe the information cultures of those specific organisations, and to tease out the various contributing factors. But in order for these findings to be of any practical use, a further step was necessary. This led to the compilation of the factors into a framework to assess or diagnose the culture in different organisations (Oliver, 2011).

Some factors appeared to be associated with national cultural differences, which means that these characteristics would be deeply embedded in the ways in which people act, and very resistant to change. On the other hand, some characteristics reflected features which appeared to be much more organisation specific, rather than country specific. These features would indeed be possible to change.

The missing piece of the puzzle came into sharper focus after discussion of information management problems with employees of a Pacific Islands nation regional body which had responsibility for providing technical advice and services for a very wide range of different specialities. There were many different sub-cultures in this particular organisation, including expatriate employees from developed countries, local hires from various Pacific Island nations, in addition to all the different occupations and professions represented. There was huge variation in people's ability to work with the technological tools available (e.g. familiarity with a shared-drive environ-ment, or coping strategies for an environment affected by frequent power outages). This really highlighted the importance of information-related competencies, including digital literacy, where there was a clear skills gap, which could be effectively addressed by training, in conjunction with the more traditional areas of training targeted by recordkeeping practitioners: knowledge and understanding of recordkeeping requirements.

The framework has subsequently been modified as a further series of case studies was conducted between 2015 and 2017 in research supported by the International Council on Archives. The modified framework, described in detail in the following chapters, is shown in Figure 1.2 opposite.

Level one is the bottom level of the pyramid. It represents those factors which are so fundamental that they are very hard to change. However, it is extremely important to find out what they are so that strategies, policies and procedures can be designed appropriately. The factors to be taken into consideration at this level are as follows:

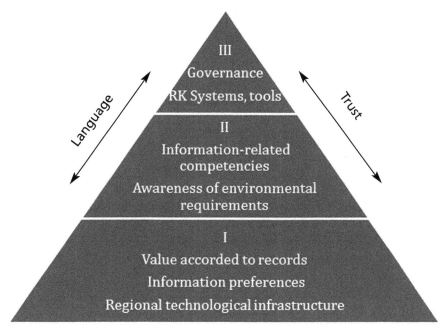

Figure 1.2 *Information Culture Framework (ICF)*

- the value accorded to records, or respect for information as evidence. Recognition and awareness of the need to manage certain information for the purposes of accountability
- preferences for different communication media and formats, as well as preferences with regard to sharing information. The former involves consideration of preferred primary sources for information; the latter, the level of granularity to which information sharing is regarded as the norm by employee
- regional technological infrastructure: the technological infrastructure in the country or region that where the organisation is located.

Respect for information as evidence is discussed in detail in Chapter 2; preferences for different media and formats, willingness to share information and differing views of which resources can be most relied on are considered in Chapter 3. Regional technological infrastructure is discussed in Chapter 4.

The second level of the pyramid represents the skills, knowledge and expertise of employees relating to information and records management, and which can be acquired and/or extended in the workplace. This is placed in the middle of the triangle because training development will take into account those fundamental influences at the bottom. The skills, knowledge and expertise can be divided into two broad categories:

- information-related competencies, including information and digital literacy
- awareness of environmental (societal and organisational) requirements relating to recordkeeping.

These categories are discussed in Chapters 5 and 6, respectively.

At the tip of the pyramid are two organisational features which are highly significant for successful recordkeeping and are the most susceptible to change. These two features are interlinked, and are considered in Chapter 7:

- the information governance model that is in place in the organisation
- recordkeeping systems and tools.

In addition, there are two metalevels, indicated by the arrows in Figure 1.2. These are concerned with language and communication, and trust in recordkeeping systems and professionals. The two metalevels are discussed in Chapter 8.

Each chapter not only identifies and describes the various components of the framework, but also provides guidance as to how to go about assessment, and then suggests what actions can be taken once that the data has been collected in order to provide a way through 'the people problem'. The sequencing of discussion in the book corresponds to levels 1, 2 and 3, followed by the metalevels – but this consecutive approach is not the only way of approaching assessment. It is possible to target just one level of the framework, as time and resources permit, and thus take a piecemeal approach to building the information culture profile. The only proviso to working in this way is to remember that the factors at other levels are present, and not to discount those influences.

The key question is, of course, why bother at all? What is so special about information culture? Why expend all this time and effort? Why not use another assessment methodology?

Why recordkeeping culture?

By focusing on 'recordkeeping cultures', rather than considering the broader and less precise notion of information culture, this second edition of our book aims to address people's values and attitudes towards the 'information objects' that represent their present and past actions. Records embody our intentions and enable us to act in the world, and be accountable for our actions. Recordkeeping is therefore essential to all social groups, from mainstream organisations to small, independent communities, as they all need records in order to act effectively and to leave a reliable trace of their pursuits.

As was emphasised in the previous edition, one of the principles guiding our approach is that there is no one way of enacting records-related values and practices, and recordkeeping environments may be as diverse as the information environments examined in our previous book. Recordkeeping cultures is therefore an inclusive notion, where diversity and multiplicity of record enactments are seen as a positive quality, while reductionism and prescriptiveness in recordkeeping behaviours are not valued as core to the archival and records management disciplines.

As argued above, organisational culture has been acknowledged to be a critical concept to be taken into account when implementing recordkeeping systems. However, organisational culture is a nebulous concept, used and defined in many different ways and thus open to significant misinter-pretation. Information culture, and, more precisely, recordkeeping culture, consciously embraces multiple layers of culture (e.g. national, occupational and corporate) and, most importantly, ensures that attention is directed to the heart of the matter, records, and yet does not ignore the underlying and encompassing organisational contextual issues. This is the key point, and one of the main differentiators between a recordkeeping-culture approach and other holistic strategies such as information audit and the information maturity model. In recent years a plethora of assessment strategies and tools have been developed – unsurprisingly, given the increasingly standards-driven nature of records management. These strategies and tools may supplement rather than replace an information culture assessment. Other holistic approaches and assessment tools are discussed in the following two sections.

Other approaches

In order to clearly differentiate the new approach afforded by the ICF, it is necessary to spend some time considering the alternatives. These include information audits and information maturity models, as well as the tools that have been developed specifically for records management: DIRKS (Designing and Implementing Recordkeeping Systems), JISC's (Joint Information Systems Committee) impact calculator and records management maturity models, and ARMA International's Generally Accepted Recordkeeping Principles (GARP).

Information audits

Information audits achieved some popularity as an organisational strategy from the early 1990s onwards and still appear to have credence with some practitioners and consultants (for example, see Leming, 2018). Susan Henczel, one of the leading exponents of information auditing, provides the following explanation:

> The information audit is a process that will effectively determine the current information environment by identifying what information is required to meet the needs of the organization. It establishes what information is currently supplied, and allows a matching of the two to identify gaps, inconsistencies and duplications. The process will also facilitate the mapping of information flows throughout the organization and between the organization and its external environment to enable the identification of bottlenecks and inefficiencies.
>
> (Henczel, 2001, 45)

Similarly, Elizabeth Orna refers to the definition adopted by ASLIB, the British professional association for information management:

> A systematic evaluation of information use, resources and flows, with a verification by reference to both people and existing documents in order to establish the extent to which they are contributing to an organization's objectives.
>
> (Orna, 1999, 69)

Despite the representation of information audits as a holistic approach to information management within organisations, neither definition appears to remotely allude to records – information as evidence – but seems to focus on information as (a source of) knowledge, for the purpose of increasing awareness.

Although Henczel refers to audit as a standardised management methodology (p.45), it has been pointed out that there is no single, standardised way of carrying out an information audit (Botha and Boon, 2003). These authors reviewed the various methodologies and concluded that the following elements, broadly interpreted, could represent a standardised approach:

- planning
- information needs assessment
- information survey

- costing and valuing information resources
- analysis
- reporting.

No doubt the scope of an audit could be stretched to include records, but the value of doing this is dubious, to say the least. The notion that records are static objects that can be inventoried is completely at odds with our world of complex and emerging digital technologies and systems. Records are evidence of business transactions, thus they are inextricably linked with actions, with doing something. Identifying and listing the outputs of activities that continue to take place as the organisation carries out its functions is a time-wasting and ultimately profitless endeavour. However, identifying and understanding the processes of the business, and making sure that knowledge reflects ongoing developments within the organisation, will provide insight into the records that need to be created and managed.

Furthermore, finding out what information is available and what the information needs of users are, will not provide any assistance in figuring out how to meet those needs – and which of those needs are needs for evidence. The essence of the information culture approach is a rich understanding of the ways in which the members of the organisation interact with information, and using this insight to develop strategies tailored to the specific context.

Information maturity models

Another holistic approach to assessing the extent to which organisations successfully work with information is the information maturity model (the JISC records-specific version of this the model is discussed in the following section). Maturity models were first developed in the 1970s–80s to assess quality management (Crosby, 1979) and capability in software engineering (Humphrey, 1988). Since then the underlying concept has been adapted to focus on various organisational features. Variations on the information maturity model are used by consultants; an open source version credited to a Gartner Group company is available online.[1] This model provides five levels for assessment of information management:

- Aware
- Reactive
- Proactive
- Managed
- Optimised,

with 'Aware' as the lowest level, signifying that there is awareness of problems but no action undertaken, and 'Optimised' as the highest, where information management is a strategic priority. The methodology used to determine information maturity is a survey based on a series of 'capability statements', which reflect either the business capabilities that the organisation wants to achieve or improve, or the data-management capabilities that are the enablers of the business capabilities. Thus, capability statements are divided into clusters such as 'single view of customer', 'privacy', data cleansing, data-collection standards, etc. Each statement is associated with a framework consisting of the following elements: Policy, Practice (Process), People/Organisation, Technology, Measurement and Compliance. Associating each question with a framework element then provides insight into the relative strengths and weaknesses of those areas.

From this brief and rather superficial description it can be seen that the methodology is very highly and tightly structured, in contrast to the information audit approach. An attempt has been made to cover all angles, and the model appears to be designed for use by consultants with specific training in this methodology rather than by practitioners. It thus certainly has the look and feel, and consequently the appeal, of a very rigorous tool that will make sense of the messy and fluid nature of organisational information management. However, it is the very complexity of the information environment that presents the critical challenges, and recognition of the different purposes for which information needs to be managed is at the heart of the matter. A holistic information management maturity model assessment of this type is unlikely to have the subtlety required to capture perceptions, deep motives and unstated goals, in order to identify the features that make up a recordkeeping culture.

However, a more expansive approach to assessing maturity however does hold some promise. A model has been developed by the cybersecurity community, designed to be applied at national, rather than organisational level (Global Cyber Security Capacity Centre, 2018a). One of the dimensions of the model is concerned with culture (Global Cyber Security Capacity Centre, 2018b), and implementation of the methodology includes interviews and focus group discussions, resulting in a rich picture of cybersecurity readiness. Outcomes from the application of the model indicate ratings for different areas according to the following categories: start-up, formative, established, strategic, and dynamic. Synergies between information cultures and cybersecurity readiness/maturity would seem to be a fruitful area for further exploration.

Other assessment tools

The recordkeeping environment has become increasingly standards driven. In keeping with this, a number of assessment tools and methodologies targeted specifically at records management have been developed. These include tools developed in Australia (DIRKS), the UK (JISC impact calculator and maturity model) and the USA (GARP). None of these tools appears to be actively supported any longer, which seems to indicate that they have been less than successful. Nonetheless, it is worth identifying and reflecting on each of these as the problems encountered provide useful pointers to future actions.

Designing and Implementing Recordkeeping Systems (DIRKS)

The forerunner of them all is the Australian methodology Designing and Implementing Recordkeeping Systems (DIRKS). This was originally developed by the public records authority in New South Wales (NSW), and then subsequently promoted and supported in partnership with the federal National Archives of Australia. There is little current information about it on current archival authority websites; a Wikipedia entry maintains that it is still in use in New South Wales, somewhat bizarrely describing it as a 'non-tool' (DIRKS, n.d.). The very detailed manual itself is still available for download from the New South Wales government website.[2]

The DIRKS methodology consists of eight stages, corresponding to system design methodology but adapted to a specifically recordkeeping environment. In essence, the methodology aims to assess the existing organisational needs for recordkeeping and then use this information in order to design a recordkeeping system. Thus specific stages are as follows:

1   preliminary investigation
2   analysis of business activity
3   identification of recordkeeping requirements
4   assessment of existing systems
5   identification of strategies for recordkeeping
6   design of a recordkeeping system
7   implementation of a recordkeeping system
8   post-implementation review.

The methodology was recognised internationally, and provided the structure for the second part of the initial version of ISO15489. However, the application of DIRKS has been problematic.

There had been a lot of anecdotal evidence over the years about difficulties experienced by organisations in implementing DIRKS, and eventually a published comment explained the situation:

> The DIRKS process model for designing and implementing record-keeping systems is a fairly straightforward, flexible, and logical model for systems implementation. Yet, the NAA managed to antagonize a large number of government agencies unnecessarily by insisting upon an overly complicated and rigid set of DIRKS implementation processes for identifying and documenting business functions and activities, and their associated record-keeping requirements. As a result, DIRKS projects were bogged down in years of glacial progress and often fruitless effort.
>
> (Cunningham, 2011, 26)

The message here is clear. Any assessment methodology, if it is to be implemented successfully by organisations, has to be relatively simple and straightforward. The more complex the process becomes, the less likely it is to be used. Furthermore, as Cunningham also points out, research has indicated that people issues are a highly significant factor to be taken into account in developing effective recordkeeping systems (p. 25).

The research that Adrian Cunningham refers to is the Accelerating Positive Change in Electronic Records Management (AC+erm) Project conducted at Northumbria University, and also referred to in the Introduction to this book. The findings are particularly significant because they represent input from the international community, and do not just reflect views from one nation or theoretical perspective. The key points from this project include the following, which are particularly germane to this discussion:

- the people, process and systems/technology aspects of ERM [electronic records management] are inextricably linked; though useful for the research design and as an analytical tool, the distinction between them is not one that can legitimately be drawn in modelling what actually happens
- people issues are predominant, fundamental and challenging as they concern culture, philosophical attitudes, awareness of RM [records management] and ERM issues, preferences, knowledge and skills
- records professionals may be part of the problem as well as part of the solution, e.g. they take the holistic view and have the principles and tools to manage records but their demands may be unrealistic or too constraining
- solutions for ERM are contextualized and complex.

(McLeod et al., 2010, 17)

An information culture approach is designed to get to the heart of those people issues which predominate, while taking into account the systems and processes involved. Gaining an in-depth understanding of the culture of the organisation will enable records professionals to take a much more realistic view of organisational life and to develop strategies that facilitate rather than constrain. Despite the marked lack of success of DIRKS there is much in it that is valuable and useful. The manual can perhaps best be used as a reference resource, for guidance on specific activities documented in ISO15489, rather than be regarded as a definitive methodology for implementation. It is referred to further in Chapter 6, where specific DIRKS steps are particularly relevant.

Impact Calculator and Records Management Maturity Model

Under the auspices of JISC InfoNet (a service providing advice and guidance on records management to the UK education sector) two tools were developed, which aim to provide empirical data on the return on investment of records management programmes. A characteristic of records management has been the lack of verifiable data to support frequently made claims such as promises for efficiency improvements or space savings. We have tended to rely on anecdotal evidence, such as spurious claims to achieve x% savings by introducing a certain storage system.

The aim of the impact calculator is described as follows:

> To assist in measuring the actual impact of a change initiative. Impact in this instance can be defined as a comparison of the measurable benefits, generally efficiency savings or gains brought about by a change initiative, and the costs incurred by implementing it. The Impact Calculator supports the collation of information relating to measurable benefits that can be quantified in both monetary and non-monetary terms.

> (Bailey, 2011, 48)

The calculator was pilot tested by six universities, each attempting to measure benefits from the implementation of a specific activity leading to change (for example, training in e-mail management). The overall findings from these pilot studies are reported by Bailey (2011), and, although he concludes by reiterating the value of the calculator, not all pilot study participants were as positive. The final report from the University of Aberdeen, for instance, notes some important concerns, namely difficulties in using the calculator for their chosen project, and the fundamental issue of records management outcomes rarely matching direct savings:

Many records managers with long experience of the profession would note that good records management does not always translate into cost savings (eg an extra square metre of space in 20 rooms does not equate to an extra 20 square metre room) and the danger of being seen as nothing more than a cost-cutter is one which can undermine the profession.

(University of Aberdeen, 2010, 2)

It appears that the Impact Calculator may have had some utility in measuring quantifiable benefits achieved in the implementation of some (but not all) change initiatives.

The other tool developed as part of this JISC initiative was the Records Management Maturity Model. The tool was developed for a very specific situation, namely to enable tertiary-sector institutions to self-assess progress towards meeting the requirements set out in the records management code of practice which accompanied the introduction of freedom of information legislation in the United Kingdom (JISC InfoNet, 2012).

The design of the model follows the general pattern described above for the Information Management Maturity Model. In this case, statements describing specific features of records management programmes are clustered into 33 distinct groups. For each statement one of four rankings can be selected:

- **0 Absent** – Institution shows no evidence of awareness of the need to take a strategic approach to the management of records;
- **1 Aware** – Uncoordinated local attempts to improve records management in response to local issues;
- **2 Defined** – Coordinated attempts to improve records management underway across the institution; and
- **3 Embedded** – The effective management of records is fully integrated within the institution's strategic and operational activities.

(JISC InfoNet, 2012)

The resulting data is calculated for each area, and an overall summary is generated which provides an overview of the stage of development of the programme. This, and similar audit tools developed for specific jurisdictions, provides an effective way of highlighting areas of strength and weakness. However, it does not provide any insight as to why these weaknesses exist, and how best to tackle them.

Generally Accepted Recordkeeping Principles (GARP)

The final evaluation method considered here was developed by the United States professional records managers' association, ARMA International. This name, GARP, was selected because of the similarity to the widely known GAAP, Generally Accepted Accounting Principles.

Once again, the underlying tool was that of a maturity model, in this case the information governance maturity model (for more on information governance see Chapter 7.) Despite ringing endorsement for GARP in the *Information Management Journal*, published by ARMA International (see, for instance, Colgan, 2011; Hoke, 2011; Susec, 2011; Whan, 2011), the tool itself does not appear to be available any longer. As with the Impact Calculator and the Records Management Maturity Model, GARP provided a way of measuring a current environment, but without providing any insight into why this is the case, or how best to go about improving the situation. In other words, the all-important nuances are not evident in these quantitative approaches to assessment. To use the language of academic research, the tools that generate numeric scores (Information Management Maturity Model, Impact Calculator, Records Management Maturity Model, GARP) stem from the positivist tradition. This view of the world considers that everything is measurable, that is, quantifiable and objectively knowable. By assuming that the reality 'out there' is subject to laws that can be discovered and verified, this research tradition attempts to apply methods used in the natural sciences to the social sciences.

The Information Audit, on the other hand, is a bit of a misfit. Despite its name there does not appear to be a standardised methodology in place, but use of the word 'audit' does imply that the intention is for checking and review, with the ultimate aim of attributing a score.

By way of contrast, the ICF offers a much more holistic view of the information environment. By taking into account influences external to the organisation and identifying cultural characteristics that, rather than be changed, have to be taken into account, it provides a means to address those 'how' and 'why' questions. In other words, it belongs in the interpretive tradition of enquiry, a tradition that privileges qualitative methods over quantitative ones, and that is primarily concerned with 'meaning'. According to this research paradigm, our social world is interpreted or constructed by people, and is therefore different from the natural world.

Summary and conclusions

The concept of information culture can be and has been applied to societies and nation-states as well as to organisations. The literature relating to organisational information culture does convey sometimes confusing and conflicting views, but in general, acknowledges linkages with organisational culture. Our standpoint is that every organisation has an information culture, and within this broader framework, every organisation has one or more recordkeeping cultures. Not all recordkeeping cultures are conducive to the kinds of 'good' records and information management that the specialised literature prescribes. How to assess or diagnose the information/record-keeping culture of individual organisations is our aim in the subsequent chapters of this book. We maintain that figuring out the characteristic features of an organisation's information culture is a crucial and essential step on the path to addressing the people problems that have proved to be the stumbling block in establishing effective records management programmes to date.

Information culture assessment needs to be undertaken in the context of understanding the nature and purpose of other approaches to assessment, such as DIRKS and maturity models. It is not proposed as a means by which metrics can be collected; rather, it should be viewed as facilitating deep understanding of a highly complex environment. The remaining chapters provide practical guidance for assessment at each of the levels of the ICF.

Notes

1 http://mike2.openmethodology.org/wiki/Information_Maturity_Model [accessed 7 November 2018].
2 Strategies for Documenting Government Business: The DIRKS Manual https://www.opengov.nsw.gov.au/publications/17383.

References

Audunson, R. and Nordlie, R. (2003). Information Literacy: the case or non-case of Norway? *Library Review*, **52** (7), 319–25.

Bailey, S. (2011) Measuring the Impact of Records Management: data and discussion from the UK higher education sector, *Records Management Journal*, **21** (1), 46–68.

Botha, H. and Boon, J. A. (2003) The Information Audit: principles and guidelines, *Libri*, **53** (1), 23–38.

Brown, D. and Starkey, K. (1994) The Effect of Organisational Culture on Communication and Information, *Journal of Management Studies*, **31** (6), 807–28.

Choo, C. W., Bergeron, P., Detlor, B. and Heaton, L. (2008) Information Culture and

Information Use: an exploratory study of three organizations, *Journal of the American Society for Information Science and Technology*, **59** (5), 792–804.

Colgan, J. J. (2011) Using GARP® to Objectively Measure your Recordkeeping Program, *Information Management Journal*, **45** (5), 38–41.

Crosby, P. B. (1979) *Quality is Free: the art of making quality certain*, Vol. 94, McGraw-Hill.

Cunningham, A. (2011) Good Digital Records Don't Just 'Happen': embedding digital recordkeeping as an organic component of business processes and systems, *Archivaria*, **71**, 21–34.

Curry, A. and Moore, C. (2003) Assessing Information Culture – an Exploratory Model, *International Journal of Information Management*, **23** (2), 91–110.

Davenport, T. H. and Prusak, L. (1997) *Information Ecology: mastering the information and knowledge environment*, Oxford University Press.

Davenport, T. H., Eccles, R. G. and Prusak, L. (1992) Information Politics, *Sloan Management Review*, Fall, 53–65.

DeSanctis, G. and Poole, M. S. (1994) Capturing the Complexity in Advanced Technology Use: adaptive structuration theory, *Organization Science*, **5** (2), 121–47

DIRKS (n.d.) https://en.wikipedia.org/wiki/DIRKS [accessed 7 November 2018]

Douglas, J. (2010) The Identification, Development and Application of Information Culture in the Western Australian Public Sector, Doctor of Philosophy, Edith Cowan University.

Foscarini, F. (2009) Function-Based Records Classification Systems: an exploratory study of records management practices in central banks, Doctor of Philosophy, University of British Columbia.

Foscarini, F. (2012) Understanding Functions: an organizational culture perspective. *Records Management Journal*, **22** (1), 20–36.

Fourman, M. (2003) Informatics. In Feather, J. and Sturges, R. P. (eds), *International Encyclopedia of Information and Library Science*, Routledge, 237–44.

Ginman, M. (1993) Information and Business Performance. In Olaisen, J. (ed.), *Information Management: a Scandinavian approach*, Scandinavian U.P., 79–94.

Global Cyber Security Capacity Centre (2018a). *Cybersecurity Capacity Model for Nations (CCMN)*, https://www.sbs.ox.ac.uk/cybersecurity-capacity/content/cybersecurity-capa city-maturity-model-nations-cmm-0 [accessed 7 November 2018]

Global Cyber Security Capacity Centre (2018b). *CMM Dimension 2 : Cyber Culture and Society*, https://www.sbs.ox.ac.uk/cybersecurity-capacity/content/cmm-dimension-2-cyber-culture-and-society [accessed 7 November 2018]

Grimshaw, A. (1995) *Information Culture and Business Performance*, University of Hertfordshire Press.

Henczel, S. (2001) *The Information Audit*, KG Saur.

Hofstede, G. (2001) *Culture's Consequences: comparing values, behaviors, institutions, and organizations across nations*, 2nd edn, Sage Publications.

Hoke, G. E. J. (2011) Shoring Up, *Information Management Journal*, **45** (1), 26–28, 30–31, 46.

Humphrey, W. S. (1989) *Managing the Software Process*, Addison-Wesley Professional.

Jarvenpaa, S. L. and Staples, D. S. (2000) The Use of Collaborative Electronic Media for Information Sharing: an exploratory study of determinants, *Journal of Strategic Information Systems*, **9**, 129–54.

Jarvenpaa, S. L. and Staples, D. S. (2001) Exploring Perceptions of Organizational Ownership of Information and Expertise, *Journal of Management Information Systems*, **18** (1), 151–83.

JISC InfoNet (2012) *Records Management Maturity Model: assess your current records management measures*, https://www.jisc.ac.uk/guides/records-management/maturity-model [accessed 7 November 2018].

Keen, A. (2007) *The Cult of the Amateur: how today's internet is killing our culture and assaulting our economy*, Nicholas Brealey.

Leming, R. (2018) *Conducting an Information Audit*, https://www.woodyfindsdata.com/infoaudit [accessed 7 November 2018].

McLeod, J., Childs, S. and Hardiman, R. (2010) *AC+erm Project (Accelerating Positive Change in Electronic Records Management) – Final Project Report*, www.northumbria.ac.uk/static/5007/ceispdf/final.pdf [accessed 13 August 2012].

Marchand, D. A., Kettinger, W. J. and Rollins, J. D. (2002) *Information Orientation: the link to business performance*, Oxford University Press.

Martin, V. A., Lycett, M. and Macredie, R. (2003) Exploring the Gap Between Business and IT: an information culture approach. Paper presented at the Action in Language, Organisations and Information Systems, Linkoping, Sweden.

Mayer-Schönberger, V. (2009) *Delete: The virtue of forgetting in the digital age*, Princeton University Press.

Nilsen, K. (1994) Government Information Policy in Canada, *Government Information Quarterly*, **11** (2), 191–209.

Oliver, G. (2008) Information Culture: exploration of differing values and attitudes to information in organisations, *Journal of Documentation*, **64** (3), 363–85.

Oliver, G. (2011) *Organisational Culture for Information Managers*, Chandos.

Oliver, G. (2014). International Records Management Standards: the challenges of achieving consensus. *Records Management Journal*, **24** (1), 22–31.

Orna, E. (1999) *Practical Information Policies*, Gower Publishing Company Limited.

Riyaz, A. and Smith, K. (2012) Information Culture in the Maldives. In Spink, A. and Singh, D. (eds), *Library and Information Science Trends and Research: Asia-Oceania*, Emerald, 173–208.

Rosenberg, V. (1982). Information Policies of Developing Countries: the case of Brazil, *Journal of the American Society for Information Science*, **33** (4), 203–7.

Susec, M. (2011) Calling 9-1-1: avoiding disaster using GARP®, *Information Management Journal*, **45** (4), 36–9, 46.

Szecskö, T. (1986) Mass Communications and the Restructuring of the Public Sphere: some aspects of the development of 'information culture' in Hungary, *Media, Culture and Society*, **8** (2), 199–210.

Tredinnick, L. (2008) *Digital Information Culture: the individual and society in the digital age*, Chandos.

University of Aberdeen (2010) *Developing and Testing Sustainable Strategies for Managing the Amount of Email, which Meet Organisational Needs While at The Same Time Satisfying the Requirements of Users: The University of Aberdeen final report*, http://issuu.com/jiscinfonet/docs/aberdeen_updated_jisc_impact_calculator [accessed 13 August 2012].

Upward, F. (1997) Structuring the Records Continuum Part Two: structuration theory and recordkeeping, *Archives and Manuscripts*, **25** (1), 10–35.

Upward, F. (2000) Modelling the Continuum as Paradigm Shift in Recordkeeping and Archiving Process, and Beyond – a Personal Reflection, *Records Management Journal*, **10** (3), 115–39.

Upward, F., Reed, B., Oliver, G. and Evans, J. (2013). Recordkeeping Informatics: re-figuring a discipline in crisis with a single minded approach, *Records Management Journal*, **23** (1), 37–50.

Upward, F., Reed, B., Oliver, G. and Evans, J. (2018). *Recordkeeping Informatics for a Networked Age*, Monash University Publishing.

Whan, C. (2011) Leveraging GARP to Ensure Employee Engagement, *Information Management Journal*, **45** (6), 32–5, 47.

Widén, G. and Hansen, P. (2012) Managing Collaborative Information Sharing: bridging research on information culture and collaborative information behaviour, *Information Research*, **17** (4), paper 538, http://informationr.net/ir/17-4/paper538.html#.UdLqG-t8M7A [accessed 13 August 2012].

Widén, G. and Karim, M. (2018) Role of Information Culture in Workplace Information Literacy: a literature review. In: Kurbanoğlu, S., Boustany, J., Špiranec, S., Grassian, E., Mizrachi, D. and Roy, L. (eds) *Information Literacy in the Workplace. ECIL 2017*. Communications in Computer and Information Science, vol. 810. Springer, Cham.

Widén-Wulff, G. (2000) Business Information Culture: a qualitative study of the information culture in the Finnish insurance industry, *Information Research*, **5** (3), http://informationr.net/ir/5-3/paper77.html [accessed 18 September 2013].

Widén-Wulff, G. and Ginman, M. (2004) Explaining Knowledge Sharing in Organizations Through the Dimensions of Social Capital, *Journal of Information Science*, **30** (5), 448–58.

Widén-Wulff, G., Ek, S., Ginman, M., Perttilä, R., Södergård, P. and Tötterman, A.-K. (2008) Information Behaviour Meets Social Capital: a conceptual model, *Journal of Information Science*, **34** (3), 346–55.

Yeo, G. (2018) *Records, Information and Data: exploring the role of record-keeping in an information culture*, Facet Publishing.

Zheng, Y. (2005) Information Culture and Development: Chinese experience of e-health, *Proceedings of the 38th Hawaii International Conference on System Sciences*, 3–6 January.

PART 2

CHAPTER 2

The value accorded to records

This chapter is the first of three that consider the level one factors of the ICF (see Figure 1.2). It deals with the area that can be the most daunting and is possibly the most challenging to tackle and to develop strategies for: the extent to which members of the organisation 'respect records'; or, to put it another way, the extent to which people accept that it is desirable and necessary to manage information as evidence, for accountability purposes. This core value will be reflected in behaviours and attitudes, in resourcing and, ultimately, in the success of the records management programme.

The chapter begins by providing some background to explain the influences that shape this value. It then describes the likely manifestation of differing values towards information as evidence, as reflected in attitudes and behaviours, the recordkeeping infrastructure and IT usage. The next section suggests various methods to use in assessment, including observation, survey and/or interviews, and provides guidance to help select which options are appropriate in different organisational environments. The concluding section, on interventions, suggests ways to develop appropriate responses, which include taking what may be perceived as radically different approaches to traditionally accepted practices.

Cultural influences

The cultural influences that shape people's thinking about information as evidence, i.e. records, are many and varied. Organisational culture theory stresses that attention should be paid to *layers of culture* – e.g. national, occupational (or professional) and corporate. This has been explored at length in previous work (Oliver, 2011; Foscarini et al., 2013), and so the main points are just briefly summarised here. Organisations and the people who work in them do not exist in a vacuum, therefore it is incorrect to assume that 'organisational culture' is an easily discernible characteristic that can be neatly categorised as good or bad, strong or weak. The geographic location of the organisation will strongly influence the way things are done, not least because of the laws, regulations and standards that govern the workplace. The industry or sector to which the organisation belongs (e.g. banking, education, health) will offer similarities in terms of approaches to recordkeeping, understandings of its purpose and any ethical considerations attached to it. Then individual employees will bring values, attitudes and behaviours to bear which have been shaped by growing up in particular environments, as well as by their previous education and training to carry out specific jobs. Overlaying these factors are the corporate values, real or aspired to, which are defined by management and can change accordingly.

An important feature to be aware of, that has achieved little prominence in records management discussions, is the susceptibility of recordkeeping activities in certain cultural contexts to management trends and fads. Two of the case studies that Fiorella conducted of the development and imple-mentation of functional classification systems in national banks highlighted this very clearly. In one bank, functions were associated with what was perceived as being a new approach to management; in another, identifying functions was associated with being an 'agile organisation' (Foscarini, 2012, 30). The concept of agile working began as a methodology for software development and has subsequently been applied to organisational contexts, underpinned by the principles of the Agile Manifesto. The twelve principles of the Manifesto do not mention the need to document activities, but do stress face-to-face communication: 'The most efficient and effective method of conveying information to and within a development team is face-to-face conversation.' (Principles behind the Agile Manifesto, n.d.).

Gillian's experience has been similar, in that records-related activities in New Zealand from the 1980s onwards appear to have been strongly influenced by Thomas Peters and Richard Waterman's populist and evangelical bestseller, *In Search of Excellence* (Oliver and Konsa, 2012). This phenomenon will be reflected in the uppermost cultural layer, that of corporate culture – but there are clear connections with the other two layers.

American information systems researchers Elena Karahanna, J. Roberto Evaristo and Mark Srite (2005) have provided an expanded notion of the cultural layers existing in any organisation by adding supranational (including regional, ethnic, religious, linguistic and other cultural differences that cross boundaries or can be seen to exist in more than one nation) and group influences (cultural characteristics that manifest within a single office, workgroup or other collection of individuals at a level less than that of the organisation) to those identified above (national, occupational and corporate). They also relate such cultural layers to two distinct types of workplace behaviour; namely, behaviours that include a strong social component and involve judgement are more likely to be influenced by national or supranational cultural characteristics, whereas behaviours that have a strong task component and involve practice rather than value considerations may be subject more to the influences of occupational (or professional), corporate or group culture.

This presents an interesting avenue for future research in recordkeeping: being able to associate specific behaviour types with the different layers of culture will provide us with significant insight. For instance, one may assume that appraising records and assigning retention periods will partly reflect value systems acquired through the family, the social context one grew up in, and later through school, while the activities involved in registering records and routing them to specific employees will be primarily influenced by workplace practices and professional skills.

The lessons that we can draw from this now are that you should not expect to find uniformity in terms of values within an organisation. As with all studies of culture, the aim is to determine the likelihood that people will hold a certain value or belief, not that all individuals will react in the same way. The more complex your organisation, the more likely it is that there will be significant variety in terms of values held.

If an organisation is a multinational corporation, then national cultural differences will almost certainly come into play. Similarly, if an organisation does business internationally, be prepared to deal with some differences in behaviours which will inevitably impact on recordkeeping. Leaving aside the possibly more easily discernible national differences, most organisations will have representatives from various occupational groups. People working in legal and audit departments are likely to have distinctly different approaches to managing records than their colleagues in forward-facing, customer service roles, for instance.

These discontinuities may also be interpreted in relation to a common distinction made by sociologists and organisational theorists between *values* and *practices*. The former have been defined as 'enduring beliefs that a specific mode of conduct […] is personally and socially preferable to an opposite or converse mode of conduct' (Rokeach, 1973, 5). The latter are more visible to an external observer and often manifest themselves in symbols, heroes and rituals (Hofstede, 2001). Values may be seen as systems of deep assumptions that have strong affective components, are acquired early on in life and tend to be rather stable (Karahanna et al., 2005, 5), while practices are attitudes that are 'learned later through socialisation at the workplace after an individual's values are firmly in place' (Karahanna et al., 2005, 6). Values and practices are two critical aspects of culture and are intertwined. Ideally, practices should reflect values, but this is not always the case. When practices dictated by one level of culture (e.g. organisational) are not aligned with the values comprising another level of culture (e.g. national), tensions and conflicts may arise.

By applying the value/practice distinction, organisational researchers have also concluded that 'shared perceptions of daily practices are the core of an organisation's culture' (Hofstede, 2001, 204). This implies, for instance, that by contributing policies and procedure for the management of the corporate record, records managers play an active role in shaping the culture of their workplace.

Despite the existence of such regulatory frameworks, people in organisations do show significant differences in the ways in which they understand and respond to recordkeeping requirements (Lewellen, 2015), and indeed whether they regard them positively or negatively. These differences reflect their underlying values relating to records, which they may not even be aware of. This area is very much a black box. We cannot predict what values will be held by which people in which settings and in which roles, because of the complexity and fluidity of the individual and environmental factors affecting the deep structure of human behaviour. However, that should not prevent us from recognising that differences exist and developing our strategies accordingly. The next three sections explore how differing values relating to records may be reflected in organisations.

Attitudes and behaviours

Given that our international standard, ISO15489, specifies that everyone has a role to play in ensuring that records are created and captured into recordkeeping systems, it is essential that all employees recognise their responsibilities in this regard. However, when you are working in an environment where respect for and understanding of records and recordkeeping processes cannot be taken for granted, or where the act of documenting is perceived as negative behaviour, the records manager can appear to be faced with insurmountable difficulties.

It may come as a surprise to records managers in Anglo-American environments that in other parts of the world there may be broad acceptance of the need to manage records. For instance, the challenges faced by Australia and New Zealand's records managers in needing to explain why it is essential for business transactions to be documented and for organisation-wide systems to be created and used simply are not present in some other countries. For example, organisations established in the new private sector in Estonia appeared to be continuing with predecessor documentation practices (Oliver and Konsa, 2012).

However, even where practices are well established and adhered to by employees with respect to the traditionally generated record formats such as letters and reports, this ingrained records 'appreciation' may not be being routinely applied to e-mails, business information systems and social media. So, although it may appear that the nature of records is clearly understood by employees, it cannot be assumed that this understanding is sophisticated enough to be routinely transferred to newer formats and systems.

The perspectives of employees or community members on records and recordkeeping (and therefore the value accorded) are likely to be manifest in the following attitudes and behaviours:

- use or non-use of recordkeeping systems (see also Chapter 8 for issues relating to trust)
- readiness to buy into recordkeeping policy
- willingness to carry out recordkeeping procedures (for instance, selecting and assigning appropriate metadata to a document)
- readiness to set up personal systems to support their work-related information needs, indicating that the use of organisational systems is for compliance purposes only
- willingness to participate in training related to records management.

Each of these bullet points should not be interpreted as a binary 'will they or won't they'. Actual behaviours can best be thought of in terms of a sliding scale. At the most negative, extreme behaviours could in fact sabotage organisational strategies – for example, removal of documents from a paper file or deliberately assigning inappropriate metadata. Moving towards the midpoint of the scale, but with just as detrimental an impact, are the casual behaviours which appear to be doing what is required, such as always selecting metadata terms from the most easily accessible ones in a drop-down list (one records manager of our acquaintance was astonished to find so many financial policy records tagged 'avocados', but quickly realised that it was because the term appeared in the first section of the list of pre-defined metadata options). At the other extreme, the most positive end of the scale, employees with a very sophisticated understanding of why records are important may be active participants in the ongoing development of recordkeeping systems, and be regarded as valuable sources of ideas and innovation.

Researchers who apply structuration theory (Giddens, 1984) to the study of the interactions between human agents and organisational structures have provided insights into employees' attitudes towards technologies that may be used to look at options listed above in a more nuanced way. For instance, the idea of 'appropriation' has been suggested as a useful concept to understand what people think of the tools the organisation provides them with, and how they actually use such tools. Groups of users of a given system or technology may choose to: (1) directly use the structures provided (e.g. group members fully comply with the rules embedded in the system); (2) relate them to other structures (e.g. group members register documents in a separate spreadsheet); (3) constrain the structures as they are used (e.g. group members adopt a local interpretation of certain metadata that is different from the 'official' one adopted by the organisation); or (4) make judgements about the structures (e.g. group members affirm or deny the usefulness of performing certain actions) (DeSanctis and Poole, 1994, 129).

By closely observing how groups behave when using a technology one may realise whether their 'appropriation moves' are 'faithful' or 'unfaithful'. According to Gerardine DeSanctis and Marshall S. Poole, two representatives of the Adaptive Structuration Theory (AST) school, when people use a technology according to its 'spirit' (that is, the technology's intended use, in line with the rules promoted by its designers) they appropriate it faithfully; and if, on the contrary, they consciously or unconsciously modify certain structural features or adapt the 'spirit' of the technology to their needs, the appropriation is unfaithful. 'Unfaithful appropriations', they explain, 'are not "bad" or "improper" but simply out of line with the spirit of the technology' (DeSanctis and Poole, 1994, 130). Besides considering whether a recordkeeping system is used or not used (see the first bullet point on p. 37), we may look deeper into the way in which it is used (i.e. faithfully or unfaithfully) and discover implicit motives, unofficial ways of working, hidden procedures that are the unwritten rules constituting actual organisational behaviours.

Recordkeeping infrastructure

Perhaps the most obvious feature that can be assumed to at least partially reflect the value accorded to records within an organisation is the nature and degree of development of the recordkeeping infrastructure. By infrastructure we mean the features that constitute and provide the framework for the recordkeeping programme; these features are one of the three diagnostic indicators used in the ICA Toolkit (see Chapter 9). Infrastructure features are likely to include the following elements:

- the employment of specialist staff, appropriate for the size and complexity of the organisation
- the existence of organisation-wide recordkeeping policies and procedures, and mechanisms (e.g. training) to enable, promote and facilitate their application
- the existence of systems appropriate for the management of both digital and paper records
- recordkeeping functionality embedded in all other business information systems.

The final two bullet points both address recordkeeping systems (for more on this see Chapter 7), but with key differences. The first encompasses those systems which are usually regarded as doing the job of records management – so, EDRMS as well as traditional hard-copy filing systems. The second point acknowledges that records creation and maintenance should not be limited only to certain document formats, but should include all business transactions carried out by the organisation. This means that when new information systems are developed and implemented, the requirements to create and maintain information as evidence must be considered. This is a much more difficult area to address and assess than the 'explicit' systems in the first category, although it is being given more prominence now with the development of MoReq2010 (Modular Requirements for Records Systems) and ICA standards (DLM Forum Foundation, 2011; International Council on Archives, 2008).

   It should be noted that at the beginning of this section we cautiously stated that the recordkeeping infrastructure may at least *partially* reflect the importance accorded to records and recordkeeping. This is because the existence of a comprehensive recordkeeping programme may in fact be due to the efforts of one or a handful of people, and not reflect the values and existing practices of the organisation or the majority of its employees. If good infrastructure is in place and the recordkeeping programme is well resourced, find out whether this has been a progressive, ongoing development over time and/or whether this can be attributed to one individual or a small group of people. Of particular concern here is whether the critical individual or group holds a leadership role in the organisation. This attribution is a key consideration, as understanding this correctly will ensure that you do not misinterpret the current situation and assume that a well-supported recordkeeping regime reflects positive values towards records throughout the organisation.

In environments where there is not a strong tradition of robust recordkeeping the employment of specialist staff and management support for the implementation of appropriate systems and processes may be solely due to the vision and persistence of a few individuals. It has certainly been Gillian's experience, consulting in New Zealand businesses, that the development and bedding in of recordkeeping programmes has been successful only when championed by an individual at senior management level. The word 'championed' is used deliberately, as this person typically provides more than just support. They can be thought of as crusaders, fighting for the cause at every opportunity. The significance of the crusaders is soon recognised when they leave the organisation. The investments made in resourcing recordkeeping will very quickly wither and die, unless a replacement crusader is identified.

IT usage: the EDRMS challenge

Many records managers will, sadly, be only too well aware of the issues and challenges associated with EDRMS. For many years these systems have been promoted as the only way in which digital records can be managed to ensure those key characteristics of authenticity, reliability, usability and integrity. Many, many problems have been experienced in the implementation and deployment of these systems. No matter how technically perfect they are as solutions, if people do not use EDRMS consistently, the systems are not fulfilling their *raison d'être*: the management of the organisation's information assets.

Employee resistance and reluctance to routinely use these systems could at least partially reflect underlying values towards records (see Lewellen, 2015 for research investigating this in the New Zealand public sector). If recordkeeping is not accepted as being of critical importance, then any additional tasks involved will be seen as an imposition, the straws breaking the camel's back.

Information systems theory has not provided much assistance with this problem, as the accepted orthodoxy is that if habits can be created, then usage will continue. There has been recognition, however, that emotions, and unplanned and apparently unreasoned actions, are likely to be very influential too (Ortiz de Guinea and Markus, 2009). In the case of EDRMS, the variation in people's understanding of and respect for records is likely to come into play. So it is important not to assume that in organisations where

EDRMS are not fully utilised, or are 'unfaithfully' used, it is simply a question of the right habits being instilled. Ways to address this particular problem area by developing training strategies are discussed in Chapter 5.

Assessment techniques

There are a number of possible techniques for assessing the value accorded to records in organisations. Using the ICA Information Toolkit (see Chapter 9) provides a holistic approach to assessment; in this section the focus is specifically on the level one value characteristic. The choices you make will be governed by the time you have available, your familiarity and comfort level with individual techniques and the complexity of your organisation. Last but not least, make sure that any pre-existing assessment work that you or your predecessors have already carried out is taken into account.

Pre-existing work is mentioned because this specific area is the one most likely to have been at least partially assessed if one of the standard tools described in Chapter 1 has been applied. The Records Management Maturity Model (JISC InfoNet, 2012), for instance, although specifically developed for UK higher education institutions to self-assess their ability to comply with freedom of information legislation, nevertheless could be used to provide insight into the nature and extent of the records management infrastructure in any organisation type, anywhere in the world. Similarly if you work in an organisation that is subject to an audit regime (for example, Archives New Zealand conducts audits of recordkeeping in public sector organisations in accordance with the Public Records Act 2005 [Archives New Zealand, 2018]) which includes review of the records management infrastructure.

The other techniques that can be used, on their own, in combination or to supplement tools such as the Records Management Maturity Model, are developing a survey, talking to people (interviews and focus groups) and observing their environment, and desk research.

As a general methodological note, it should be emphasised that the approach we suggest in this book, and that underlies the Toolkit described in Chapter 9, is primarily inquisitive or exploratory, that is, it is not meant to *solve problems* but, rather, to understand *what the problems are* and how to improve the 'problem situation' (Checkland and Scholes, 1999). This stance comes from the belief shared by the authors that problem-solving methods are not very effective when it comes to dealing with 'soft', unstructured issues – as most issues involving human beings are. For instance, while engineers are allowed to concern themselves with solutions ('what is to be'), because the problems they face tend to be rather structured (e.g. how to build a bridge in the most effective, efficient and economic way), records managers, and generally all professionals who cannot ignore the *social context* in which people act, need first of all to understand what goes on, the 'what is' question (Checkland, 1999, 126). This way of thinking, also known as 'soft systems thinking' (as opposed to the 'hard systems thinking' typical of the natural sciences), was translated into a methodology for the social sciences known as Soft Systems Methodology by Peter Checkland and others.

Another way to characterise the methodological approach best suited for this kind of research is to refer to the world of ethnography, although, given the limitations inherent in most studies of organisational contexts (e.g. time constraints, inaccessibility of resources), ethnographic techniques may not be fully available to the researcher (see Oliver et al., 2018). The ethnographic aspiration of information culture studies, as it emerges particularly when conducting interviews and observations, is explained later in this chapter and in Chapter 8.

Developing a survey

Developing a survey, online if possible, is an efficient means of collecting information from a large number of people, spread across a geographically diverse organisation. However, people today are in danger of being over-surveyed – which can and often does result in reluctance to participate. We are frequently requested to participate in surveys in our professional lives to support research activities, not to mention requests for our input on everything from the state of the nation's political parties to what we thought about the last hotel we stayed at. So, if you do decide to develop a survey, a lot of thought has to go into making sure that you gain the maximum response rate. Key considerations are the following:

1 The survey should be as short and focused as possible. Don't include any unnecessary questions that won't provide insight into the values accorded to records.
2 Questions should be as simple as possible to respond to. If you can provide true/false, multiple choice answers or a Lickert scale (a range of options such as Always/Often/Sometimes/Never/Not Applicable) to get the information you need, do so. People are much more likely to respond to a survey when responding entails just one click, rather than having to write text. In addition, the simpler the answer, the easier it is to collate the responses.
3 Offer an incentive, such as a spot prize for a completed survey form.

4 Provide assurance that responses will be at least confidential, if not anonymous. You want to find out what attitudes and behaviours are practised, but if these contradict organisational policy, users may be reluctant to be honest.
5 Use an online survey tool if possible. This will make life much easier for both you and your respondents. Distribution will be simply a matter of e-mailing a link to users, and much of the data analysis (if not all) can be done by generating a report from the software.
6 Provide feedback. There's nothing worse than spending time answering survey questions and then never finding out any outcome. If you successfully develop the art of compiling small and tightly focused surveys, the chances are that you will use this tool often, so don't abuse the goodwill of your respondents.

Sample questions

The questions should be designed to find out how people view their roles and responsibilities in the records management process, so possible questions can include asking for responses to the following statements:

- Recordkeeping is everyone's responsibility: True/False/Don't Know
- Recordkeeping requirements are a barrier to working efficiently: Always/Often/Sometimes/Never/Not Applicable
- Recordkeeping is an essential part of my work: Always/Often/Sometimes/Never/Not Applicable
- I make sure all my work-related e-mails are filed appropriately: Always/Often/Sometimes/Never/Not Applicable

The language used for these questions should be tailored accordingly, so that it refers to the systems that are currently in place. For instance, it may be more pertinent to ask about tagging e-mails with metadata, rather than 'filing' them in some settings.

Conducting interviews

Talking and, just as importantly, listening to people is the best way to gain deep understanding of their attitudes and behaviours with regard to records and recordkeeping. An additional benefit is that engaging directly with your users will assist in building supportive networks and good relationships. The downside of interviewing is that it is time intensive; whether you are able to use interviews to gather all the information you need will depend on the size and complexity of your workplace. Furthermore, the resulting data (the comments and discussion made by interviewees) is more difficult to collate and present than the numbers and percentages gained from questionnaires.

The potential for insight derived from interviewing people and the difficulties involved were the key motivators for us to develop a toolkit for practitioners. The toolkit provides a methodology to develop an information profile for a particular setting; the steps involved are described in Chapter 9.

Selecting interviewees and scheduling the interviews are important factors. You should aim to speak to people who use, as well as those who don't use, existing systems. It will also be important to make sure that employees from all levels of the organisation are included in your sample, in order to make sure that you are not getting just the views from, say, the management perspective. Similarly, make sure that all departments or work units are represented.

Interviews should be scheduled at times most convenient for your interviewees. Do not underestimate the complexity of finding mutually convenient times and places – once you embark on this process it can be extremely time consuming, as people's obligations change and new priorities surface.

One way of minimising the time required for individual interviews and the problems associated with scheduling them is to conduct group interviews, or focus group discussions. In this approach, rather than having one-on-one conversations with individuals, you will hold sessions with small groups. Groups should be carefully constituted. For example, it may be appropriate to form groups of all individuals with a given role or at a given level within the organisation. Alternatively, it may work better if groups are from the same team or department. In the latter instance, though, think carefully about whether people working at a lower level will be willing to speak their mind and possibly contradict their managerial colleagues in open discussion.

The downside of working with groups is that it needs a lot of skill to be able to lead discussion, keep things on track (i.e. stick to the topic), make sure that all have the opportunity to voice their opinions and, on top of all that, to take notes as well. Digitally recording the sessions may seem an easy way to address that last difficulty, but bear in mind that will mean subsequent listening and note taking. The preferred option would be to use an experienced facilitator to run sessions, and for the records manager to be in a listening and note-taking role throughout. Keeping the groups small will help; more than five or six individuals participating may well prove to be unmanageable.

Especially when studying your own organisation (and also more generally when conducting this kind of empirical research) you may not be able to detach yourself from your way of looking at things – in other words, your subjectivity – so you may easily become 'deaf' to what people tell you during the interview. It is important to be aware of your biases and not to pretend to be a 'neutral' investigator. Conducting interviews together with some colleagues might help to avoid your interpretative framework getting in the way and distorting the perspectives of your interviewees.

Interview guide

Before embarking on any interview session, whether one-on-one or group, it is important to have prepared an interview plan or guide. This will usually consist of a list of indicative questions to act as a reminder for the interviewer of the areas that need to be covered. However, unlike the questionnaire, interviews should be flexible enough to allow the interviewer to pursue themes that emerge from responses, and to allow discussion. The toolkit includes an interview guide which addresses all levels of the ICF (see Chapter 9). If additional questions to probe people's respect for records and recordkeeping are required, we suggest the following:

- What do you think about the statement 'Recordkeeping is everyone's responsibility'?
- Would you agree with the proposition 'Recordkeeping requirements are a barrier to working efficiently'? Why, or why not?
- Do you see recordkeeping as an essential part of your work? Why or why not?

Each of these questions can be explored in much more depth if you come prepared with examples, that is, recordkeeping procedures that are likely to be linked to the interviewee's position, such as whether they are conscious of the need to add e-mails to the corporate system, and whether activities such as this are viewed as reasonable and justifiable.

Desk research

'Desk research' is used throughout this book as a comprehensive term to encompass all those data-gathering activities that do not include direct contact with people. As a matter of principle we do emphasise the importance of engaging directly with users, but do not forget about the other sources of information which can also be used. In order to assess the value that employees assign to records, documentary analysis, transaction log analysis and observation are all valid techniques.

Documentary analysis

This involves checking certain key organisational documents for records management-related requirements. For instance, do position descriptions and/or performance agreements for non-specialist records management staff include reference to recordkeeping responsibilities? Has recordkeeping policy been formulated and promulgated throughout the organisation? Does other organisational policy make reference to recordkeeping perspectives when relevant (for instance, business continuity or disaster management plans, risk management strategies)? Some of these factors may well be covered if you have used an existing standard tool, such as a maturity model or audit, so don't forget to check back to the findings of such exercises if you have already gone down that path.

Transaction log analysis

Statistics relating to the usage of IT systems can be gleaned from the transaction logs that record system activity. This information is generally available only to systems administrators, so if you have not been assigned those privileges for recordkeeping systems such as an EDRMS then it will be necessary to find out who does, and then request access to this data. Transaction logs may reveal patterns of usage across the organisation, showing which areas of the organisation are active users of the recordkeeping system and which are not. Depending on the system used, the transaction data may be customisable, so this is a very important area to investigate and make use of.

Observation

This technique can be applied in two ways, one more direct and less resource hungry (i.e. observing what is in existence in terms of infrastructure) and the other requiring a certain subtlety, as it involves being able to 'see' (observe and interpret) the 'deep meaning' of everyday objects and actions, that is, things that would normally tend to pass unnoticed.

The first type of observation is a very viable technique if very little development has occurred, which is generally the case if recordkeeping is a new function within the organisation. The much more time-consuming use of a maturity-model type of tool is really not necessary when it is clearly evident that there is no organisation-wide classification system, or no EDRMS and so on. It is only when these things exist that a more nuanced view (considering to what extent specific features are effective) becomes useful.

Observations of the second type are common in ethnographic studies, where the observer immerses him- or herself in the reality of the subjects under investigation in order to try to capture the meanings of what they do (for more on ethnography see Chapter 8). By adopting a simplified version, this technique may be usefully applied by non-ethnographers as well. For instance, observing where the recordkeeping unit is located within an organisation (e.g. is it in the basement or next to the president office? What kind of furniture is in the records manager's office? How are individual spaces arranged?) may provide interesting insights into the social status accorded to records managers in the organisation and, consequently, the values attached to the corporate record. Artefacts are never neutral. Actions can have symbolic meanings too. In languages where there is a distinction between informal and formal personal pronouns (e.g. in German, *du* and *Sie*; in French, *tu* and *vous*) observing how employees address one another may have implications in terms of their preferences for informal versus formal means of communication, trust and attitudes towards sharing.

Interventions

Once you have determined the values of your users as regards the need or importance of keeping records, you have achieved major progress because you now have key information that you need in order to communicate and work effectively. You will need to develop two main approaches. The first concerns language, the second concerns readiness to make a fundamental shift away from traditional records management practice.

Speak their language

It is critically important to speak the language of your users. As discussed above, it is very unlikely that a homogeneous approach is going to work for your users. Key messages will have to be tailored accordingly. This does appear to make life more complicated, so it is essential that records managers have a deep understanding of their mission and purpose. Having that deep understanding means that you will be able to use language that is appropriate for your non-specialist colleagues, but without losing sight of what it is you have to achieve.

For instance, if 'records' are interpreted by employees as something tedious and bureaucratic associated with the paper world, then by all means use 'information' instead. However, be prepared to provide lots of examples so as to be very clear about the types of information you are concerned with, together with instances to explain why this is important. As is discussed in Chapter 8, language is a pervasive cultural element that influences all kinds of interactions, and it cannot therefore be associated with only one level of the ICF.

Be open to new approaches

It's time to start thinking and acting outside the box. If you are working in an environment where respect for records cannot be assumed as a given, then very little will be achieved by insisting that users follow procedures that do not mesh with the ways in which they work. Fiorella's research has also shown that lack of understanding of a holistic approach to organising records is by no means limited to environments characterised by flat-structured organisations. On the contrary, this absence of understanding was also apparent in the organisations that supposedly represented 'ideal' record-keeping environments, i.e. full bureaucracies.

A recurring theme throughout this book is the suggestion of new ways of doing things. For instance, we suggest approaching training needs from a very different perspective, that of information and digital literacy skills (see Chapter 5). Another example of a new approach is to borrow and apply ideas from genre studies, to ensure that users' viewpoints and the way that they work are acknowledged and reflected in systems that are developed for records managers. In earlier work Fiorella has described this as one of several 'soft' approaches to records management (another one is Soft Systems Methodology, see p. 42), in contrast to sets of 'hard' methods that tend to be more common in current recordkeeping environments (Foscarini, 2010). Taking a genre perspective will involve looking at how people adapt formal procedures and customise them to the way they work, and will require stepping back from our insistence on one right, official way of doing things and allowing users to participate in designing systems and processes. We explain more about genre ideas in Chapter 9.

Yet another proposed new approach involves applying human computer–interaction (HCI) principles and strategies (Bailey and Vidyarthi, 2010). This should include consideration of how recordkeeping could be more enjoyable and less painful for everyone involved. Information systems literature may provide insight into this area, as described by Weimei Pan (2017).

One very practical action that can be taken now that does not require any specialist knowledge or technical expertise is to establish a recordkeeping governance board or committee. It should include representation from all functional areas and is a key mechanism to start developing mutual respect and understanding across the organisation. The purpose of the board would be to provide the records manager with guidance, advice and support. The records manager would use the board to test and develop new policies and procedures, thus facilitating the growth of a participatory and consultative environment. Trying to impose new ways of working and doing things in the absence of this setting is doomed to failure, particularly in those organisations where recognition of the value of records and recordkeeping is likely to be low or non-existent.

Summary and conclusions

Table 2.1 summarises the key features that need to be examined in order to assess the value accorded to records in an organisation, and links them with specific assessment techniques.

Table 2.1 *Features reflecting values accorded to records, and assessment techniques*

Feature	Assessment technique
Recordkeeping infrastructure	1 Existing tool, e.g. Records Management Maturity Model or Audit Tool 2 Desk research – observation 3 Desk research – documentary analysis (records management policy)
Attitudes and behaviours	1 Questionnaire 2 Conducting interviews 3 Desk research – documentary analysis (position descriptions) 4 Desk research – documentary analysis (acknowledgement of records management requirements in other organisational policy)
IT usage	1 Desk research – data log analysis 2 Conducting interviews

Decide which of the approaches in Table 2.1 to apply, with a view to answering the following questions:

- Do the employees of my organisation tend to have a high or low respect for records and recordkeeping?
- Is there significant variation in respect across the organisation? If so, can this be associated with particular work units and/or locations?

You will probably need to dip into more than one of the assessment techniques. The aim is not to collect definitive data characterising individuals, but to gain a feel for the value accorded to records by the users of recordkeeping systems in given settings. This information will be used, in conjunction with other ICF findings, to help you understand your organisation's recordkeeping culture and, eventually, to develop and implement strategies to improve it. The value accorded to records is a critical factor that will shape training programmes, and this is discussed in Part Two. The next chapter considers further ICF level one factors: information preferences.

References

Archives New Zealand (2018) Audit Self Assessment, http://audit.archives.govt.nz/;jsessionid=E4C5BEC7203E5328E4FD96D7EF0975CF.app1 [accessed 22 December 2018].

Bailey, S. and Vidyarthi, J. (2010) Human-Computer Interaction: the missing piece of the records management puzzle? *Records Management Journal*, **20** (3), 279–90.

Checkland, P. (1999) *System Thinking, System Practice*, John Wiley & Sons Ltd.

Checkland, P. and Scholes, J. (1999) *Soft Systems Methodology in Action*, John Wiley & Sons Ltd.

DeSanctis, G. and Poole, M. S. (1994) Capturing the Complexity in Advanced Technology Use: adaptive structuration theory, *Organization Science*, **5** (2), 121–47.

DLM Forum Foundation, *MoReq2010®: Modular Requirements for Records Systems – Volume 1: Core Services & Plug-in Modules* (2011) http://moreq2010.eu/ [accessed 21 December 2012].

Foscarini, F. (2010) Understanding the Context of Records Creation and Use: 'Hard' versus 'soft' approaches to records management, *Archival Science*, **10**, 389–407.

Foscarini, F. (2012) Understanding Functions: an organizational culture perspective, *Records Management Journal*, **22** (1), 20–36.

Foscarini, F., Oliver, G., Ilerbaig, J. and Krumrei, K. (2013) Preservation Cultures: developing a framework for a culturally sensitive digital preservation agenda, *Proceedings of the UNESCO Conference: The Memory of the World in the Digital Age: Digitization and Preservation. Vancouver, September 26–28, 2012*, UNESCO, 419–30.

Giddens, A. (1984) *The Constitution of Society: outline of the theory of structuration*, University of California Press.

Hofstede, G. (2001) *Culture's Consequences: comparing values, behaviors, institutions, and organizations across nations,* 2nd edn, Sage Publications.

International Council on Archives (2008) *Principles and Functional Requirements for Records in Electronic Office Environments. Module 3 Guidelines and functional requirements for records in business systems,* http://adri.gov.au/products/ICA-M3-BS.pdf [accessed 21 December 2012].

JISC InfoNet (2012) *Records Management Maturity Model: assess your current records management measures,* www.jiscinfonet.ac.uk/tools/maturity-model/ [accessed 21 December 2012].

Karahanna, E., Evaristo, J. R. and Srite, M. (2005) Levels of Culture and Individual Behaviour: an integrative perspective, *Journal of Global Information Management,* **13** (3), 1–20.

Lewellen, M. J. (2015) The Impact of the Perceived Value of Records on the Use of Electronic Recordkeeping Systems. PhD, Victoria University of Wellington.

Oliver, G. (2011) *Organisational Culture for Information Managers,* Chandos.

Oliver, G. and Konsa, K. (2012) Dismantling Bureaucracies: consequences for recordkeeping in New Zealand and in Estonia, *Journal of the Society of Archivists,* **33** (1), 89–108.

Oliver, G., Foscarini, F., Sinclair, C., Nicholls, C. and Loriente, L. (2018) Ethnographic Sensitivity and Current Recordkeeping: applying information culture analysis in the workplace, *Records Management Journal* **28** (2), 175–186.

Ortiz de Guinea, A. and Markus, M. L. (2009) Why Break the Habit of a Lifetime? Rethinking the roles of intention, habit, and emotion in continuing information technology use, *MIS Quarterly,* **33** (3), 433–44.

Pan, W. (2017) The Implementation of Electronic Recordkeeping Systems: an exploratory study of socio-technical issues, *Records Management Journal,* **27** (1), 84–98.

Principles behind the Agile Manifesto (n.d.) http://agilemanifesto.org/principles.html [accessed 22 December 2018]

Rokeach, M. (1973) *The Nature of Human Values,* Free Press.

CHAPTER 3

Information preferences

This chapter discusses two fundamental information preferences which are key characteristics to assess at ICF level one (see Figure 1.2). The first preference is a complex cluster of factors which are often overlooked entirely. It encompasses differences in terms of need for explicit versus implicit information in order to communicate successfully, as well as variation in tendencies to prefer (or trust) written rather than informal sources of information communicated by individuals in one's own social group, and vice versa.

The second preference is a phenomenon which has been much more widely studied, namely, willingness to share information and the level of granularity to which it is felt to be appropriate to share (e.g. with colleagues in the same workgroup). Just as with the value accorded to records, discussed in the preceding chapter, these preferences lead to information behaviours that are essential to identify but difficult if not impossible to change. Underlying these behaviours may be issues of trust, which are discussed further in Chapter 8.

While influencing these subjective choices is usually quite difficult, as the reasons for preferring one course of action over another may reside very deep in one's subconscious, what records managers and other information experts can change are the conditions within which carrying out certain choices may become possible. These kinds of interventions relate to information governance, which is the subject of Chapter 7.

This chapter begins by attempting to disentangle the cluster of preferences relating to different sources and formats of information, and suggests reasons for preferences for textual (in all its many variants) or oral communication channels, linking these to different cultural traditions. The next section considers preferences relating to sharing information, and discusses the association of these with different national cultures, as well as with occupational and corporate cultural features.

Assessment methods that are appropriate for identifying these information preferences centre mostly on identification of the dimensions of national culture that are likely to be influential. In contrast to the interviews and surveys discussed in the previous chapter, this approach will be relatively straightforward and much less time intensive. In order to identify local drivers that will impact on information sharing, it will also be necessary to undertake some analysis of organisational documents. The concluding section on interventions urges consideration of alternative, non-traditional record formats, and emphasises the need to take into account any organisational requirements to safeguard confidential information, both within the organisation and in relation to external stakeholders, in the design of recordkeeping programmes and systems.

Words or pictures?

Recordkeeping is traditionally assumed to be concerned with the written record. The cluster of factors discussed in this section raises awareness of innate preferences for other formats and sources of information. Recognition of a range of preferences will help to ensure that differing perspectives can be taken into account when designing systems and procedures and in developing training. It is important to escape the one-size-fits-all mentality, and the assumption that everyone will have the same internalised view of what 'best practice' constitutes. Key factors are the variation in:

- preferences relating to the form and manner in which information is communicated
- perceptions of what constitutes an authoritative information resource.

The rise and rise of the written word

In Chapter 1 we highlighted some of the main trends in the discussion and debate of information culture from a societal perspective. Analysis has charted the major technological trends which have impacted on literacy, ranging from the introduction of the printing press in the 15th century, through the development of mass media and on to today's increasing reliance on new textual forms such as those created on social media. Luke Tredinnick provides an in-depth analysis of the changing face of textual communication, making reference to Walter Ong's claim for the development of a secondary orality in the 20th century, due to the rise of media such as radio and telephone, which lessened the importance of written communication (Ong,

1982, 3). Tredinnick argues that subsequently, with the emergence of digital technologies, writing has regained importance, albeit in ways which lead to vastly different manifestations of language, reproducibility, malleability and questions about the very nature of authenticity (2008, 59–78) which are at the heart of current concerns about fake news in a post-truth society. An early exploration of issues relating to authenticity was undertaken from an archival perspective by Canadian archivist Hugh Taylor (1988).

Authenticity is a key concern for records managers; the international standard on records management, ISO15489, states very clearly that authenticity is an essential characteristic for records (ISO, 2016). But, as much as assessing what is an original and what is a copy in the digital world, establishing and protecting the authenticity of electronic records is a challenge that has attracted the attention of leading researchers in archival science, with perhaps the best-known centre of activity being the InterPARES 1 project (Duranti, 2005).

On a less theoretical and more practical level, the emergence of new forms and means of communicating via the written word are undoubtedly relevant to any consideration of records management. Practitioners grapple with the nitty-gritty of the 'how to' questions when new technological tools are used to conduct business. These questions indeed often seem to dominate the professional discourse as represented on national online discussion forums whether in the UK's RECORDS-MANAGEMENT-UK list, the USA's RECMGMT-L or New Zealand's NZRecords; how do we manage text messages, what do we do about online chat, and so on, are key recurring topics.

However, this concern with shifting trends and patterns in the use of technologies and their impact on textual communication is firmly grounded in the context of the Western world and does not take into account differing cultural traditions and their associated preferences for oral, pictorial or non-textual communication. This is not a trivial point, as these preferences will fundamentally influence whether and how records are created, and also how records will be consulted and used. Ultimately, whether textual records will necessarily be regarded as more authoritative and comprehensive than other sources of information cannot be assumed to be uniform across all cultural traditions.

Another phenomenon that is changing textual versus non-textual preferences on a global scale has to do with the ease of taking and sharing images (e.g. photos, emojis) through instant messaging apps. Why would you spend time and mental energy to describe in words a situation you are witnessing when you could take a picture of it, capture it as a video or be offered by your mobile device a pictographic character that represents your feelings about the situation, and share it instantly? In addition to the increasing use of oral communication channels through voice messaging, this trend to replace written words with still or moving images and sounds is impacting on the relevance of textual records in contemporary societies.

Media/format preferences and cultural differences

Cultural and communication theorists have explored different preferences for oral, pictorial or written communication, and one school of thought associates them with low-context and high-context cultures. One of the most frequently referred-to models is that developed by Edward and Mildred Hall (1989). This relatively simple model relies on a single continuum of high to low context to plot cultural differences. At the high-context extreme, the emphasis is on the context rather than the content – communication takes place based not just on what is explicitly stated. The explicit content may be a minor source of information in comparison to the contextual information inherent in the person and/or environment. So, pictures and images could be much more effective than text in situations where the preference is for high-context communication. At the other end of the scale, low context indicates that the reverse situation applies. In this case, as much information as possible has to be *made explicit* for communication to be successful.

Another feature of the Halls' model is variations in attitude to time, with monochronicity (paying attention to one thing at a time) at one extreme and polychronicity (paying attention to many things at once) at the other. This is of interest, as it may influence preferences for the use of asynchronous as opposed to synchronous communication channels (for example, e-mail [asynchronous] as opposed to online chat [synchronous]).

Media richness theory (Daft and Lengel, 1986) suggests a similar positioning of media along a continuum from face-to-face interactions at the 'rich' end (characterised by the highest degree of ambiguity), through telephone communication and personally addressed letters to standardised, quantitative written reports at the 'lean' end (i.e. unequivocal messages). The rise of web-based communication has necessarily altered this model, while confirming its validity in addressing and supporting media choice in organisational contexts (Kishi, 2008). For example, with the introduction of internet access that allows for audio and video manipulation of messages, text messaging can be considered a rich medium, while the Daft and Lengel model (1986) would rank it as a lean channel. Because of its significant impact on interactivity, social media can be used by organisations to promote organisational cohesion. As such, according to Ishii et al. (2019), platforms such as Google Docs and Facebook should be classified as rich media. Despite these issues, most media scholars recognise that media richness theory is still foundational when examining continuously evolving communication technologies and media use behaviour.

Drawing on empirical data, Geert Hofstede (2001) developed a comprehensive model of culture based on the combination of a number of dimensions which reflect different cultural values. These dimensions are: power distance, uncertainty avoidance, individualism/collectivism, masculinity/femininity and long-term versus short-term orientation. Following on from the Hall model, Hofstede also identified low- and high-context characteristics and associated low context with individualism and high context with collectivism. The individualism dimension measures the extent to which a society views individualism as a positive or negative trait. The USA is at one end of the individualism scale, closely followed by Australia. The other extreme, collectivism, is characteristic of China and South-East Asian countries.[1]

The features discussed above are summarised in Table 3.1.

Table 3.1 *Summary of preferences for different media and formats associated with specific environments*

	Preferences	Environment
Choice of media	Synchronous communication, rich medium	Polychronic, collectivist cultures
	Asynchronous communication, lean medium	Monochronic, individualist cultures
Choice of format	Visual information	High context, collectivist cultures
	Predominantly text	Low context, individualist cultures

These preferences are further discussed in Chapter 5, as they are very important to take into account when developing approaches to training.

Indigenous oral traditions

The literature discussed above focuses on national cultural differences in the developed world, without taking into account indigenous cultures. Consequently, oral information traditions are not discussed in any of these models. Those of us who live and work in colonised countries with minority indigenous populations are able to witness the persistence and resilience of oral information traditions within societies that are predominantly text based. Preferences for oral transmission of information may also be apparent in work environments – for example, by relying on tribal elders to relay decisions made at meetings to the broader community, rather than (or in addition to) communicating in writing.

What's authoritative?

In the European continent, until the Middle Ages – and partly still today in common law countries – the oral testimony of witnesses used to have more weight than written testimony in the courts of law. Only when literacy became more diffused and the notary profession achieved a higher status in society, did trust in the written document start to grow. At some point (e.g. at the beginning of the 13th century in medieval Italy) written texts achieved a level of authoritativeness that made the presence of witnesses to support their authenticity less necessary (Petrucci, 1995).

Returning to our cultural theorists, it has been argued that people from low-context, individualistic countries are more likely to perceive textual information as being authoritative, whereas people from countries categorised as collectivist, or high-context countries, will prefer to place their trust in information gleaned from their personal relationships (see for example, Morden, 1999). However, it would be misleading to assume that preferences for information sources can be solely explained by differences associated with individualism and collectivism, as preferences for formal versus informal working and communication undoubtedly also come into play. Hence, in case studies that Gillian undertook in Hong Kong and Australia staff working in both those environments showed a clear preference for consulting with colleagues when asked about specific policies, rather than for checking the official written record. In the case of the Hong Kong organisation this behaviour appeared to fit with a collectivist approach to working. In the Australian workplace it was more likely to be associated with quite an informal approach to work (perhaps a symptom of the lack of respect for records discussed in the previous chapter), or it may also reflect a low ranking in terms of another of Hofstede's dimensions, power distance.

Much further research is needed to be able to definitively associate specific cultural settings with these different preferences for information type. However, we can recognise that these distinct and fundamental differences exist, and factor them into our thinking. See 'Determining national cultural dimensions' (p. 62) for more detail about the dimensions, and Table 3.2 for suggested linkages with information preferences.

Sharing information

The advent of information and communication technologies and ease in making information more widely available has drawn the attention of researchers to motivators for sharing or hoarding information. A seminal article in this domain documents the findings of US academics David Constant, Sara Kiesler and Lee Sproull and the development of a theory of information sharing (1994). The fact that this article has been cited hundreds of times since its publication shows the ongoing interest and concern in this particular problem area – because it *is* undoubtedly a problem area, one that refuses to go away, as the tensions associated with information hoarding are generally diametrically opposed to the aspirations of information systems designers.

The importance of information sharing for knowledge creation in organisations is well understood by knowledge management scholars. Nonaka and Takeuchi (1995) explained how tacit knowledge (i.e. informal knowledge that is in people's heads) is transformed into explicit knowledge (i.e. formal knowledge embedded in rules, technologies, etc.) and back again, through a recursive model – known as the SECI model: socialisation, externalisation, combination and internalisation – that relies on the existence of a certain level of internal sharing of information. The social processes that allow organisations to generate new knowledge, be innovative and prosper can take place only when people share experiences, thoughts and written texts. In the socialisation mode, tacit knowledge is transferred from an experienced person to a colleague by the two working side by side, sharing the same work and social setting. Externalisation (the process of converting tacit into explicit knowledge) happens through dialogue and collective reflection. Combination is a process of creating explicit knowledge by finding and bringing together a number of oral and written sources. Finally, internalisation means that the individual takes the experiences gained through the other modes of knowledge creation and transforms them into shared mental models or work practices (Choo, 2006). However, recognising the benefits of information sharing is not enough; other factors, including people's willingness to share what they know, need to be brought to the table.

Another approach to information sharing that is being addressed by information science researchers focuses on information behaviours in group work (see Sonnenwald, 2006). Most recently these ideas have been considered in conjunction with information culture with a view to understanding the relationship between information culture and collaborative information handling (Widén and Hansen, 2012). Our approach is that information-sharing preferences are a feature of information culture and that successful recordkeeping can be implemented only when these preferences are diagnosed and understood.

Information ownership

In the recordkeeping world the problems associated with getting people to make their information accessible in organisational systems are often addressed in terms of *information ownership*. The antecedents of this thinking can be traced to David Constant et al., who argued that belief in organisational ownership encourages information sharing with colleagues (Constant et al., 1994).

Hence, discussion usually centres on getting people to acknowledge that the records they create (or should be creating) and maintain belong to the organisation rather than themselves or the department, office, team they work for. Consequently, recordkeeping advice generally emphasises the importance of communicating to users that they should not regard the documents they create as their personal information. This is well intentioned and perfectly correct, but it can be misleading because it ignores an important underlying preference that impacts on the extent to which individuals recognise the need to share information with others.

Growing capabilities to share information and the correlation of this to changes in power and dominance have been demonstrated over the centuries. Over time we can see this pattern repeated again and again, in different settings and environments, but characterised by struggles for dominance and control of information. The difference today is the speed with which power is accumulated through the control of information – social media sites such as Facebook are a prime example of this. This big picture is an important reminder of the extent to which we humans recognise that knowledge, or information, is power. Thus, motivators to share information with others are likely to be culturally conditioned and will be influenced by the traditions and practices of the societies that we grew up in.

Information sharing and national cultural differences

Hofstede's model of cultural dimensions suggests that willingness to share information with work colleagues is associated with the individualism– collectivism dimension. People living and working in countries which are more likely to be at the collectivist end of the scale – i.e. at the opposite end to the highly individualistic USA and Australia – will be more inclined to share information with their immediate workgroup. However, this tendency should not be assumed to extend to a propensity to share information with colleagues in the same organisation who are not part of their team. This was vividly illustrated in a case study conducted in Hong Kong, when it was explained by respondents that it was not acceptable to expect to be able to access the information relating to the work of other departments and teams. If access to that information was needed, then permission had to be requested at managerial level. In contrast, though, work-related information was freely shared between members of the same team.

Rewarding hoarding

In addition to these deep-seated instinctive behaviours, the jobs that we have and the contexts that we work in can also profoundly affect the extent to which we are willing to share information with our colleagues in the workplace. In many cases job-performance and reward systems actively encourage information hoarding. Sales and consultancy roles will often focus on building relationships with specific clients in order to nurture and grow ongoing business opportunities. This type of working environment generally leads to intense competitive behaviour between employees, where those who win are the ones who have carefully guarded their client-related information so as not to allow any poaching on their territories. The greater the rewards at stake, the more information will be kept secret – and, as success in this environment is usually linked to ongoing employment, it can be seen that there is a lot at stake.

People working in other types of roles which have confidentiality requirements will also be very aware of the need to protect their information. For example, in health care or social services case management, or where work is classified as secret or confidential. But this environment is quite different to the competitive one, and the obligations to protect information are moral or legislative rather than personally motivated. In Fiorella's study of records management practices in central banks a widespread reluctance to share information emerged as an issue that affected, among other aspects of recordkeeping, the successful adoption of function-based records classification systems, independently of the geographic location of the organisations examined. Information security concerns and highly restrictive document access rules, combined with an overall competitive environment, appeared to have contributed to the establishment of a 'silo mentality' that could hardly be altered by any efforts made by information professionals to implement collaboration tools or policies meant to promote transparency (Foscarini, 2012).

Records managers are (or should be), by nature of their occupation and training, more conscious of the advantages of sharing information and, at the same time, of the need to protect information in areas where it is mandated by society to do so. However, we must also recognise the personal and industry-based drivers to hoard and hide, and not discount them because they do not fit with the categories of information that should be made available or need to be protected from a societal standpoint. Explicit societal and organisational requirements relating to records management are further discussed in Chapter 6.

Assessment techniques

The techniques to use to assess information preferences can include some of those already discussed in Chapter 2. However, a major difference is that it is unlikely that any of the pre-existing records/information management tools and methodologies described in Chapter 1 will address the preferences discussed in this chapter. Information sharing may be the exception, but if this topic is covered it is unlikely to provide you with the insights needed to determine motivations and behaviours. The key approaches all come under the heading of desk research. Focusing directly on cultural features provides one starting point.

Determining national cultural dimensions

As national culture appears to be a significant influence in shaping information preferences, we can make use of the work done by cultural theorists, in particular Geert Hofstede, to find out which dimensions will characterise our users. For more information on Hofstede's ideas about culture and the dimensions themselves, the best place to start is the book written for a general audience *Cultures and Organizations: software of the mind* (Hofstede et al., 2010). For academic researchers, the source to use is *Culture's Consequences* (Hofstede, 2001), which sets out the actual data collected and detailed conclusions drawn from it. However, it is not essential to do a lot of background reading to apply Hofstede's theory to your workplace.

The Hofstede Insights website[2] provides easy and instant access to the dimension values for over 70 different countries and allows comparisons between up to three countries. It is important to remember the need to avoid stereotyping. The scores for the different dimensions indicate a likelihood to behave in a certain way – they must not be taken to mean that everyone in a given country will be culturally 'programmed' to think and act the same way. Additionally, given the multicultural character of today's society, and consequently the presence of people having heterogeneous regional, ethnic, religious and linguistic backgrounds in almost every country and organisation, it might be useful to relate some characteristics that Hofstede places at the national level to the supranational cultural layer discussed in Chapter 2.

So, with that in mind, go ahead and work out what values are typical of the place you live and work in, by going to the Hofstede Insights website and selecting a country from the drop-down list. If your country is not listed, check to see that your area is not represented by a regional grouping, or look for a country that is likely to be similar in terms of values.

When you have selected a country you will see a bar chart showing values for the different dimensions and a brief analysis of the scores for each. Select a second country from the same drop-down menu, and you will get an immediate visual comparison showing differences and similarities in values.

Interpreting the scores for the different dimensions in terms of the information preferences discussed in this chapter is not cut and dried. Although Hofstede's dimensions have been applied to many other domains there have been few attempts to consider their effect on information practices. The three dimensions that appear to be most relevant to information are the following:

1 Individualism/collectivism: this is the extent to which a society views individualism as a positive or negative trait. Collectivism is the opposite extreme to individualism.
2 Power distance: the underlying issue is inequality, and how this is perceived by participants, or how people exercise their authority (e.g. centralisation versus decentralisation). For instance, the extent to which it is considered acceptable to disagree with the boss. High power distance indicates broad acceptance of power structures.
3 Uncertainty avoidance: this measures the degree of formalisation existing in society and is related to the extent to which people will seek to minimise uncertainty about the future. In organisations, technology, rules and rituals are mechanisms commonly used to this purpose. A high value for this dimension indicates that the need to avoid uncertainty about the future is very important for a given group.

Using Hofstede's observations of the likely differences in workplaces (2001) and our own case study experiences we can suggest associations between information preferences and dimension rankings, as shown in Table 3.2 on the next page.

Pay particular attention to any extreme contrasts between national cultural characteristics. These signal areas are where you really should be prepared

Table 3.2 *Information preferences related to Hofstede's dimensions*

	Collectivist	Individualist	High power distance	Low power distance	High uncertainty avoidance	Low uncertainty avoidance
Preference for visual information	Yes					
Preference for text		Yes				
Preference (trust) in the written, as opposed to the spoken, word			Yes		Yes	
Preference for rich medium (ambiguity)	Yes					Yes
Preference for lean medium (unam-biguousness)		Yes			Yes	
Reliance (trust) in oral information from own social network	Yes			Yes		Yes
Willingness to share information	Yes – with members of same group			Yes		

to see notable differences in behaviours. By anticipating and understanding these you will be much better placed to avoid trying to impose ways of working which are really at odds with different cultural traditions, and to modify your expectations accordingly. However, remember that national cultural traditions are just one factor at play in relation to sharing information, so the next stage is to determine what job-related features may also be present.

Identifying occupational culture influences

To find out what influences will be brought to bear on tendencies to hoard or share information in particular it will be necessary to determine firstly whether performance appraisal systems reward and encourage competitive behaviour, and secondly whether there are any organisational functions which necessitate the protection of information for legal, operational or moral reasons.

In Chapter 7 we consider the security settings of the information technology infrastructure in the organisation, which may (or may not) reflect the above features. But our current focus is at a much deeper level, and without this level one perspective we will not be able to assess the appropriateness of security settings at level three.

Key questions to answer in order to shed light on occupational culture influences on information sharing relate to the nature of the organisation and work practices. If there is a client- or customer-facing aspect, how are clients managed? Are individual employees assigned as case managers? How is successful case management measured? If targets are set, are these for teams or individuals? What are the rewards for meeting targets? What are the consequences for not meeting them? The more the focus is on individual achievements, the greater the rewards and the more severe the consequences, the more individuals will be motivated to hoard information relating to their clients, on the basis that knowledge is power.

Other organisational reasons for guarding information rather than sharing it with colleagues should be clearly evident. Is there work ongoing on issues which have commercial sensitivity, such as new product development? Are there client confidentiality issues which need to be respected?

Documentary analysis

Answers to these questions can be determined from desk research – by reading vision and mission statements, by analysing position descriptions and performance review policies.

Using a survey

General comments relating to using surveys to collect information are in Chapter 2. In the interests of minimising the burden on users and maintaining goodwill, it is not likely to be necessary to question users directly about their information preferences. This is because the information you need can probably largely be gleaned by using the sources described above for insight into national and occupational factors. However, if your organisation is very multicultural, that is, has employees from a wide range of different national ethnicities, you could consider developing an initial question or two relating to their background. As mentioned earlier, Hofstede's dimensions can easily be reinterpreted as factors that work at the supranational level as well. The following are examples of questions that may help you to get a better picture of your respondents' backgrounds:

- Please select up to two countries that you have lived and worked in [from a drop-down list]
- How long have you worked in [this country]? Less than five years/Five to ten years/Over ten years?

However, some words of warning. This type of question ventures into areas that people may be very sensitive about. Consult with your human resources department before attempting this, and proceed only if approval is granted. (If you are working in a country with a minority indigenous population there may well be employment statistics already available organisationally.) After all, the purpose of this activity is to promote uptake of and participation in recordkeeping, not to engender suspicion and mistrust. If you do go ahead, as we emphasised in Chapter 2, be very careful to stress the anonymity of responses, and also be sure to explain clearly why you are trying to collect this information, how you will use it and who will have access to it.

Transaction log analysis

Finally, audit logs showing information systems transactions may also provide useful information, particularly relating to preferences for different sources of information. If organisational policies and procedures are available online, usage statistics may provide insight into whether they are frequently or ever consulted. If they are not, this may indicate reliance on colleagues and verbal advice rather than regarding a written document as the only authoritative source of information. This cannot be conclusively established, as other factors relating to ease of use and retrievability come into play, but it can be considered a possible indicator. Investigating policy awareness is discussed further in Chapter 6.

Interventions

The emergence of new technological forms means that records managers should be alert to different ways of creating and sharing records, and therefore the possibilities of catering for a range of different information preferences. The ubiquitous smartphones and tablets, for example, mean that video recording is easily and readily available for many people. The problems and issues associated with video-recording information as evidence for accountability are immense and should not be overlooked (for instance, how to ensure that a digital recording can be preserved as trustworthy evidence for as long as needed, and addressing privacy concerns, to name just two), but that does not mean that these options should not be considered.

In Chapter 2 we mentioned genre studies as providing the basis for a new approach. This entails being alert to the information practices of your users, which may reflect different information preferences and then working out how to incorporate those perspectives into recordkeeping systems. One example is the use of 'stickies', those ubiquitous, often yellow, sticky notes used to flag issues or act as prompts. Agile software development teams will often use a task management board with stickies as a central communication channel or artefact. For instance, 'Scrum artefacts' are described as being 'specifically designed to maximise transparency of key information needed to ensure Scrum Teams are successful in delivering a "Done" Increment' (Schwaber and Sutherland, 2011, 12). These boards are immediate, visual and dynamic – and thus facilitate openness and flexibility on the part of development teams. Key decisions and developments can be captured by taking photos of the boards at key points in time determined in consultation with the development team.

Records managers must be open to new ways and means, and be prepared to keep abreast of technological enhancements to ensure that practice keeps pace with developments. If the plurality of information formats are not recognised as 'official records', then it is quite certain that the plurality of information preferences will not be addressed, and at least some users will be excluded from records management systems.

The insight you have gained into preferences for sharing information will be used to inform decision making about information governance, which is discussed in Chapter 7. For now, it can be brought to bear when determining how to promote uptake of records management systems. If you are working in an organisation that has significant drivers not to share information freely with colleagues, whether those drivers relate to national or to occupational culture, you are advised not to urge participation based on organisation-wide accessibility. Those benefits will be perceived as significant disincentives, and there will not be positive outcomes for records management.

Summary and conclusions

Table 3.3 on the next page summarises the range of information preferences discussed in this chapter, together with the assessment techniques that can be used.

Table 3.3 *Information preferences related to assessment techniques*

Preference	Assessment technique
Visual information	1. National culture – Hofstede's dimensions 2. Questionnaire
Written information	1. National culture – Hofstede's dimensions 2. Questionnaire
Reliance on social network or written documents as authoritative sources of information	1. National culture – Hofstede's dimensions 2. Transaction log analysis 3. Questionnaire
Synchronous or asynchronous communication of information	1. National culture – Hofstede's dimensions 2. Transaction log analysis 3. Questionnaire
Rich/lean medium	1. National culture – Hofstede's dimensions 2. Questionnaire
Information sharing	1. National culture – Hofstede's dimensions 2. Documentary analysis – position descriptions, mission statements, performance appraisal systems

Using Hofstede's dimensions will provide a quick and easy – but also oversimplified – way of figuring out the main information preferences that are likely to be significant influences. Supplementing this profiling activity with the job-related factors which will be evident from documentary analysis is the next major contributor to insight. Transaction log analysis and questionnaires may also be used if required. This analysis will enable you to answer key questions about your recordkeeping culture, namely the following:

• How important is it to encourage and facilitate the creation of records in non-traditional formats?
• Will emphasising information access and retrievability be seen as a threat, or a disincentive to using organisational systems?
• Will promoting a recordkeeping system as the authoritative source for information be an effective strategy?

As with the information about the values accorded to records discussed in Chapter 2, the aim of this assessment activity is not to collect definitive data about the information preferences of individual employees. The aim is to gain an overview of the prevalence of a variety of preferences among the users of recordkeeping systems in a given workplace. This information will be used in conjunction with other ICF findings to develop and implement a recordkeeping culture, and will be particularly important to take into consideration when developing training approaches and programmes. The next chapter considers the final ICF level one factor: the technological infrastructure of the country in which the organisation is situated.

Notes

1   Readers should be warned that although Hofstede's model has been widely cited by many authors from a number of different disciplines the shortcomings of his approach are almost always mentioned as well. Hofstede's limitations mainly refer to his simplistic understanding of what constitutes a nation and his deterministic view of the relationship between nations or organisations, on the one hand, and cultural characteristics, on the other. For a comprehensive critique of Hofstede's approach, see Baskerville (2003).
2   https://www.hofstede-insights.com/product/compare-countries/

References

Baskerville, R. F. (2003) Hofstede Never Studies Culture, *Accounting Organizations and Society*, **28** (1), 1–14.

Choo, C. W. (2006) *The Knowing Organization: how organizations use information to construct meaning, create knowledge, and make decisions*, 2nd edn, Oxford University Press.

Constant, D., Kiesler, S. and Sproull, L. (1994) What's Mine is Ours, or is it? A study of attitudes about information sharing, *Information Systems Research*, **5** (4), 400–21.

Daft, R. L. and Lengel, R. H. (1986) Organizational Information Media Richness Requirements, and Structural Design, *Management Science*, **32**, 554–71.

Duranti, L. (ed.) (2005) *The Long-Term Preservation of Authentic Electronic Records: findings of the InterPARES Project*, Archilab, www.interpares.org/book/index.cfm [accessed 11 February 2013].

Foscarini, F. (2012) Understanding Functions: an organizational culture perspective, *Records Management Journal*, **22** (1) 20–36.

Hall, E. T. and Hall, M. R. (1989) *Understanding Cultural Differences*, Intercultural Press.

Hofstede, G. (2001) *Culture's Consequences: comparing values, behaviors, institutions, and organizations across nations*, 2nd edn, Sage Publications.

Hofstede, G., Hofstede, G. J. and Minkov, M. (2010) *Cultures and Organizations: software of the mind*, 3rd edn, McGraw-Hill.

International Organization for Standardization (ISO) (2016) ISO15489-1:2016 Information and documentation – Records management. Part 1: Concepts and principles, 2nd edn.

Ishii, K., Madison Lyons, M. and Carr, S. A. (2019) Revisiting Media Richness Theory for Today and Future, *Human Behaviour and Emerging Technologies*, **1**, 124–31.

Kishi, M. (2008) Perceptions and Use of Electronic Media: testing the relationship between organizational interpretation differences and media richness, *Information & Management*, **45**, 281–7.

Morden, T. (1999) Models of National Culture – A Management Review, *Cross Cultural Management: An International Journal*, **6** (1), 19–44.

Nonaka, I. and Takeuchi, H. (1995) *The Knowledge-creating Company: how Japanese companies create the dynamics of innovation*, Oxford University Press.

Ong, W. (1982) *Orality and Literacy: the technology of the word*, Methuen.

Petrucci, A. (1995) The Illusion of Authentic History: documentary evidence. In: Radding, C. M. (ed. and transl.), *Writers and Readers in Medieval Italy: studies in the history of written culture*, Yale University Press, 236–50.

Schwaber, J. and Sutherland, K. (2011) *The Scrum Guide*, www.scrum.org/Portals/0/Documents/Scrum%20Guides/Scrum_Guide.pdf#zoom=100 [accessed 11 February 2013].

Sonnenwald, D.H. (2006) Challenges in Information Sharing Effectively: examples from command and control, *Information Research*, **11** (4), http://informationr.net/ir/11-4/paper270.html [accessed 11 February 2013].

Taylor, H. (1988) My Very Act and Deed: some reflections on the role of textual records in the conduct of affairs, *The American Archivist*, **51**, 456–69.

Tredinnick, L. (2008) *Digital Information Culture: the individual and society in the digital age*, Chandos.

Widén, G. and Hansen, P. (2012) Managing Collaborative Information Sharing: bridging research on information culture and collaborative information behaviour, *Information Research*, **17** (4), http://informationr.net/ir/17-4/paper538.html#.UNzyP3fyTTs [accessed 11 February 2013].

CHAPTER 4

Regional technological infrastructure

The focus of this chapter is on the final level one factor of the ICF (see Figure 1.2): the technological infrastructure that allows people and organisations to interconnect at the regional level. This is linked to a cultural layer known as 'supranational', which involves 'cultural differences that cross boundaries or can be seen to exist in more than one nation' (Karahanna et al., 2005, 5). Some of these cultural differences may not belong to more than one country or portion of a country at any point in time (for example, restrictions to internet access established at a national level); however, political and geographical borders can potentially change and, when they do so, often change quite rapidly, which is why we refer to these features as supranational.

We are still dealing with ICF level one, which means that the features we examine here are deeply rooted in specific socio-historical contexts and can hardly be modified through planned human intervention. People migrations and, more generally, phenomena of globalisation of products, ideas and other aspects of culture have an impact on such supranational factors. However, their consequences tend to manifest over long periods of time and must be taken into account when working across borders or developing international strategies such as standards.

The chapter considers the telecommunication services (primarily the internet) and the hardware and software products that constitute the technological infrastructure we all depend on as creators and users of digital information. The main factors influencing this broad infrastructure are reviewed and used as a basis to discuss possible future scenarios.

In the sections on assessment methods and interventions you will learn how to apply assessment techniques already identified in the previous chapters in order to find out what information and communication technologies (ICTs) are available in different regions.

Dealing with your organisation's broader technological context

While Chapter 7 discusses technological capabilities and strategies established at the organisational level – that is, corporate IT governance issues which are highly susceptible to change based on internal decisions, and which affect employees' work practices from within – this chapter deals with the technological enablers and constraints about which you and your organisation cannot really do anything, as they lie outside your control:, for instance, the broadband service that is available in your region, or the internet accessibility established by your government.

This broader ICT infrastructure has a great impact on the life of every one of us and the communities we inhabit, as most of the activities that are conducted in today's 'global society' depend on our ability to access information and connect with others online. Can we really not do anything about it? Of course, we can. As citizens and taxpayers we do have the possibility to influence our government's decisions, particularly when we live in democratic countries. Protest movements all over the world have demonstrated how social media can be used as a powerful tool to involve masses of people in organised actions to request important changes in society.

Furthermore, if we look at the ICT infrastructure from a socio-technical perspective – a perspective that examines the ways that human agency and technologies co-produce each other, but avoids privileging either the social or technical aspects as determining the other – we may come to the conclusion that any technological tools or systems are socially constructed. As a socio-technical achievement, the ICT infrastructure that surrounds and conditions our lives is subject to continuous negotiations and is less a 'material phenomenon' than it might appear. It actually has strong ideological and rhetorical connotations, despite the 'neutrality' with which it is usually represented.

ICT infrastructure components and influencing factors

In this section we review the primary components of an ICT infrastructure and some of the most significant factors that influence the provision and use of ICT services. Given the range and complexity of each factor, we will mostly present them as 'facts'; however, there always are deeper political, cultural and historical motives that would need to be further investigated so as to be able to fully evaluate the situations described.

Telecommunications

Contemporary telecommunication technologies include telephone, radio, fibre optics, satellites, the internet and any other electrical and electromagnetic means of communication. Because of its pervasiveness and importance for the management of written records in today's networked environment, some of the issues related to the internet will be examined separately.

A country's *economy* will of course have a major impact on the availability and affordability of telecommunication equipment. In the first edition of this book we referenced the Economist Intelligence Unit (EIU) forecast that predicted: 'by 2013 China will have become the world's second largest IT market, overtaking Japan' (EIU, 2010, 9). If one thinks that at the beginning of the 1990s China was 'a nation with virtually no connectivity' and has now become 'the world's largest market for both fixed-line and mobile telephony' (p. 10), one would expect that the penetration rates of ICTs in that country might soon reach the levels of more advanced economies. In reality, other factors should be taken into account to assess the developments of a country's technological infrastructure.

To continue with the Chinese example, the 2010 report by the EIU revealed that 'over 50% of China's population still live in relatively poor rural areas, and many rural dwellers are still unable to afford to buy a mobile phone or subscribe to telecoms services, no matter how cheap they become' (p. 10).

The *urban–rural divide* is evident in Western countries as well. As an example, the Estonian government has made huge investments to bring fast broadband services to rural areas. This, coupled with relatively prosperous households and businesses, has positioned Estonia (together with Finland and Qatar) in the 'middle tier' in terms of broadband markets, with the ambition to 'connect more than 90% of [its] population to [fast broadband] services by 2015' (EIU, 2013, 4).

Research analysts who study technological and economic trends have foreseen that mobile access and markets for content and services (including cloud computing) will in the near future help the most disadvantaged countries to get the basic services they currently lack (e.g. services for banking, health, education and transportation) (EIU, 2013, 6). Their analyses do not usually consider the risks that are inherent in 'immaterial' access and storage, particularly in relation to information ownership, security and preservation. For an examination of the main advantages and disadvantages of cloud computing, see Chapter 7.

Internet

The internet is seen as a great opportunity to foster economic growth. In 2018 it was estimated that half the global population had access to the internet, forecast to rise to three quarters by 2022 (EIU, 2018). For this reason, most governments are keen to encourage internet use and to support the computer industry and computer ownership in their countries. E-commerce and online banking are pervasive phenomena that have contributed to engender new forms of trust relationships (Cook et al., 2009 and see also Chapter 8). At the same time, some governments fear the internet's subversive potential and have been using sophisticated filters to block 'undesirable' websites and users. This is the case, for instance, in Iran, where internet censorship has been increasing since 2006.

After the initial disclosures of confidential information made by WikiLeaks in 2010, all states have come to realise that their 'secrets' are no longer protected when they are entrusted to invisible, online third parties. This awareness is going to change the internet landscape in ways that are hard to predict. For sure, the various and inconsistent legislative frameworks that currently regulate the use of the internet are no longer sustainable. Privacy, security, access and control in online environments are interrelated issues that legislative bodies in all countries need to address in a harmonised way. Whatever unified policy might be issued, it will likely affect the social dimension of the internet as a free space where people can freely express themselves.

Hardware and software

The hardware and software industry is dominated by a few powerful, USA-based companies. Despite the resulting global uniformity, compatibility and interoperability among different systems or different versions of the same system still represent a huge problem. Preserving digital records created through those systems is tremendously challenging, and authenticity is the property that is most at risk in the digital environment (Duranti, 2005).

Nevertheless, long-term preservation and record authenticity issues are not going to stop individuals and organisations from relying on electronic devices to create, use and store digital memory. However, awareness of the vulnerability of the current ICT infrastructure can influence hardware and software choices. In 2013, following the revelations of global surveillance programmes by the US National Security Agency (NSA), the Russian ministries and agencies responsible for state security and defence decided to resort to traditional typewriters to avert the theft of classified information.[1] Is this a sign that the world may be going back to paper-based communications? This is very unlikely, although, for documents containing highly sensitive data, nothing can be as secure as the old-fashioned typewriter and a sheet of paper. This example is just to illustrate how external factors may impact on people's behaviour in relation to the making and keeping of their documents.

Assessment techniques

In order to investigate technology from a social constructionist or socio-technical perspective, researchers often employ ethnographic methods. We explain how to apply ethnography to the study of your own organisation in Chapter 8. Here we review assessment techniques that have already been described in previous chapters. Surveys, interviews and documentary analyses are good starting points for acquiring a critical understanding of the main subject of this chapter. In the following pages you will learn what a 'scenario' is and how to include it in your survey tool.

Assessing your regional technological infrastructure

Various official resources are available to explore your and other countries' ICT infrastructures. A very valuable one is the EIU, which has already been cited in this chapter and whose publications can be accessed at www.eiu.com. The EIU generates quite comprehensive technology country reports, some of which are freely downloadable.

Another way of exploring this subject is by identifying national strategy documents that describe how countries intend to use ICTs to deliver services to their citizens. For instance, New Zealand's Digital Government Strategy is available online at https://www.digital.govt.nz/digital-government/strategy/strategy-summary/.

Surveys and interviews appear particularly useful if you want to explore people's perceptions of risk in relation to online environments. The following is an example of a scenario-based question that addresses this issue.

'Please pick the statement that describes more closely your work situation:

1 The risks involved by the mobility and online access provided by the new digital technologies are a small price to pay for the convenience and efficiency they provide.
2 The risks involved in the mobility and online access provided by the new digital technologies are too big a price to pay for the convenience and efficiency they provide.'

Interventions

Wide and easy access to digital materials online, and the lack of harmonised policies concerning information privacy and control over the web, pose serious cybersecurity threats. The EU addressed some of these concerns by issuing a General Data Protection Regulation (GDPR) (European Union, 2016), which came into force in May 2018. The GDPR's goal is to protect the personal data of individuals more effectively than any previous privacy legislation did, by means of harmonising data privacy regulations across the EU. Companies that have no physical presence in the EU must comply with the GDPR, too. If you offer products to EU citizens or collect 'information related to an identified or identifiable natural person' in the EU, you are subject to the GDPR. It is too early to say whether the new regulation has made companies that operate on the internet more virtuous. It has been reported that as of January 2020 only one third of organisations would be compliant with the GDPR.[2]

The international information and records professionals' community now has the important duty to understand how it can contribute to the GDPR's application, and how the GDPR impacts on its own processes and controls in relation to local archival and records management laws. The GDPR will not be the last and definitive answer to the multiple issues raised by the digital, pervasive environments in which we are immersed. Given their long-standing expertise in relevant areas, archivists and records managers should be involved in any projects dealing with any present and future frameworks to govern the internet. Being invited to the table where these issues are discussed also depends on us and our ability to show that our perspective matters.

Summary and conclusions

This chapter has offered an overview of an important factor that conditions (but does not determine) records making and keeping in organisations: the broader technological framework that enables communicating and using most of the digital objects that are created nowadays. Because it is deeply rooted in a socio-cultural layer we might tend to take technology for granted, or to think of it as something completely out of our control. But greater awareness of the role played by technology in society will help in influencing and understanding its development and use.

Notes

1   www.bbc.co.uk/news/world-europe-23282308 [accessed 20 January 2020].

2   https://www.zdnet.com/article/gdpr-160000-data-breaches-reported-already-so-expect-the-big-fines-to-follow/ [accessed 20 January 2020].

References

Cook, K. S., Levi M. and Hardin, R. (2009) *Whom Can We Trust? How groups, networks, and institutions make trust possible*, Russell Sage Foundation.

Duranti, L. (ed.) (2005) *The Long-Term Preservation of Authentic Electronic Records: findings of the InterPARES Project*, Archilab, www.interpares.org/book/index.cfm [accessed 11 February 2013].

Economist Intelligence Unit (EIU) (2010) *Industry Report: telecoms and technology China*, The Economist Intelligence Unit Ltd, https://www.eiu.com/n/ [accessed 2 July 2013].

EIU (2013) *Broadband Business Opportunities: analysis of national broadband strategies in 57 countries*, The Economist Intelligence Unit Ltd, www.eiuresources.com/Broadband2013/ [accessed 2 July 2013].

EIU (2018). *Technological readiness report*, The Economist Intelligence Unit Ltd, http://www.eiu.com/Handlers/WhitepaperHandler.ashx?fi=Technological_readiness_report.pdf&mode=wp&campaignid=TechReadiness [accessed 13 Apr 2020]

European Union (2016) Regulation (EU) 2016/679 of the European Parliament and of the Council of 27 April 2016 on the Protection of Natural Persons with Regard to the Processing of Personal Data and on the Free Movement of Such Data, and Repealing Directive 95/46/EC (General Data Protection Regulation), *Official Journal of the European Union*, L119, 4.5.2016, https://ec.europa.eu/commission/priorities/justice-and-fundamental-rights/data-protection/2018-reform-eu-data-protection-rules_en [accessed 17 March 2020].

FOLDOC (Free On-Line Dictionary of Computing) (2002) 'Record', http://foldoc.org/record [accessed 30 May 2013].

Foscarini, F. (2009) *Function-Based Records Classification Systems: an exploratory study of records management practices in central banks*, Doctor of Philosophy, University of British Columbia.

Foscarini, F. (2012) Diplomatics and Genre Theory as Complementary Approaches, *Archival Science* **12** (4), 389–409.

Geertz, C. (1983) *Local Knowledge*, Basic Books.

Hofstede, G. (2001) *Culture's Consequences: comparing values, behaviors, institutions, and organizations across nations*, 2nd edn, Sage Publications.

International Organization for Standardization (ISO) (2001) ISO15489-1:2001 Information and documentation – Records management. Part 1: General.

Karahanna, E., Evaristo, J. R. and Srite, M. (2005) Levels of Culture and Individual Behavior: an integrative perspective, *Journal of Global Information Management*, **13** (2), 1–20.

PART 3

CHAPTER 5

Information-related competencies

This chapter is the first of two that consider the knowledge, skills and expertise that individual employees required in order to carry out their records management responsibilities – the factors are identified at level two of the ICF (see Figure 2.1). Two main components of this information expertise can be distinguished: *information-related competencies* and *awareness of environmental requirements* (a.k.a. legislative/regulatory awareness). The latter is the subject of the next chapter.

Information and digital literacy skills are essential prerequisites for the development of a diffuse recordkeeping culture in organisations. The purview of this area is very wide ranging, from general skills such as the ability to deal with information overload, to the particular training needs associated with specific systems. In keeping with the increasing blurring of the boundaries between work and social life, digital literacy skills in particular will encompass competencies in a broad range of activities.

The chapter begins with discussion of the need to provide training for employees, and the issues and challenges faced in doing so. This is followed by an explanation of the two main perspectives that can be used in relation to recordkeeping training, information and digital literacy. Suggestions for using issues and concerns in these broad areas to focus on recordkeeping responsibilities include dealing with information overload, use of social media and digital continuity. Assessment techniques at level two of the ICF should preferably be undertaken in collaboration with others within the organisation, but suggestions for a solely recordkeeping approach are included here. The section on interventions suggests ways in which training content can be presented, including using employees' need for skills to manage their personal digital lives as a means of communicating key recordkeeping concepts.

The 'how to' of training is discussed in Chapter 6.

The training imperative

There is no question about the need for records managers to be actively involved in providing training to other members of their organisations. The international standard on records management, ISO15489, unequivocally emphasises that the practitioners charged with managing records programmes are not the only ones with duties and responsibilities relating to the creation and maintenance of records. The standard states that:

> [recordkeeping] responsibilities should be designated to all personnel who create and use records as part of their work, and be reflected in job descriptions and similar statements, where appropriate.
>
> (ISO15489-1, 6.3)

This is because not only is everyone in the course of their daily work likely to be involved in activities that generate information that needs to be managed as evidence, but also most of them will be directly involved in the creation of that information, without recourse to intermediaries. For instance, it is exceptional nowadays for a member of staff not to be writing and receiving e-mails – and most of those e-mails will be work related and thus require management as records. Consequently, much time and attention is (or should be) paid to the development of training programmes for everyone contributing to the work of the organisation, as directed by the international standard:

> People with assigned responsibilities relating to the creation, capture and management of records should be competent to perform these tasks. Competence should be regularly evaluated and training programs to develop and improve such competencies and skills should be designed and implemented where required.
>
> (ISO15489, 6.5)

Training is therefore particularly challenging, given the potentially wide range of roles (including volunteers and contractors) spanning the organisational hierarchy. Not surprisingly, a very focused approach to training is normally undertaken, emphasising specifically records-related concepts such as what is a record, what procedures have to be followed and so forth. A consequence of such a 'specialistic approach', is that organisational members may develop the feeling that 'doing records management' is somehow a separate activity, something they are expected to do when they are not carrying out their tasks, rather than something that is part of their regular activities.

Taking an information culture approach provides a much broader perspective and will enable the development of training that will meet recordkeeping objectives and have a universal resonance. The aim is to develop training programmes that will complement and enhance employees' ability to do their job by working efficiently and effectively with information, regardless of their role or status within the organisation.

Existing approaches to training

Records managers generally attempt to address the problematic aspect of ensuring that users play their part in recordkeeping by developing procedures that must be followed, and these then become the focus of training. But experiences with lack of user engagement with EDRMS have shown that developing new tasks seemingly unrelated to an employee's core business activities will not meet with overwhelming success or user acceptance.

What is critical now is to demonstrate that we have learned from this experience and to develop more innovative approaches. The importance of doing this can be seen by referring to another example from the broader debate on societal information culture. Viktor Mayer-Schönberger proposes a strategy of assigning expiration dates to information in order to reintroduce the notion of forgetting into our digital society, which we can easily see would be doomed to failure because of its inherent reliance on the individual. He envisions expiration dates as being assigned as metadata by the individual creating the information. Somewhat naively, he explains:

> Expiration dates are not about imposed forgetting. They are about awareness and human action, and about asking humans to reflect – if only for a few moments – how long the information they want to store may remain valuable and useful.
>
> (Mayer-Schönberger, 2009, 172)

The underlying premise is that people will willingly spend a little extra time to think about and decide on a retention period for information in the course of their normal activities. The reality, most practitioners would agree, is often diametrically opposed to this idealistic view – and our attempts to train people to behave otherwise generally fail.

Once again, the discussion at the level of societal information culture shows how concerns that are very relevant to recordkeeping goals and objectives are being considered, but without reference to the disciplinary knowledge and experience that we have accumulated. This emphasises the importance of recordkeeping professionals taking a more proactive and engaged role, but this will happen only if we can develop a deeper and more nuanced view of information handling in organisations. In other words, this is further encouragement to adopt an information culture perspective. Records managers' knowledge, understanding and experience of what so often appears to be completely cavalier behaviour towards information on the part of individual employees could provide critical input into the development of any organisational strategy shaped by the rather idealistic approach suggested above.

At the same time, thinking about our training goals from a broader perspective will provide us with the means to achieve our objectives in ways which will help to demonstrate their relevance and appropriateness to everyday life. For this reason, we argue that it is only by considering the knowledge, skills and expertise of employees in relation to information practices generally that training specific to recordkeeping can be developed.

Information-related competencies

Information-related competencies is a phrase coined by Finnish academic Reijo Savolainen as an umbrella term for all types of information-related literacies (Savolainen, 2002). It can be loosely interpreted as having the knowledge or competence to work with information regardless of its format or medium. The two main manifestations of information-related competencies that are relevant to the workplace can be categorised as *information literacy* and *digital literacy*. People's existing information-related competencies are instrumental to their abilities to understand and carry out their recordkeeping responsibilities. Similarly, our understanding of the dimensions of information literacy and digital literacy is invaluable in developing training that meets recordkeeping objectives, which can be seen as clearly relevant to everyday life rather than an unnecessary extra set of tasks to be fulfilled. A brief explanation of the two concepts follows, and examples for using them as a means to develop targeted training are given in the section on interventions.

Information literacy

Information literacy has long been a concern of the library and information science discipline. Much of the attention is focused on developing information literacy skills in schools and higher education, but there is also a growing body of work associated with information literacy in the workplace (Widén and Karim, 2018 provide a comprehensive literature review of this topic). The goal of information literacy in the workplace has been described as being to produce:

> workers who have the capacity to recognize and understand the central place that information, its creation, production, reproduction, circulation, and dissemination play in sustainable workplace performance.
>
> (Lloyd, 2011, 280)

Not surprisingly, the focus of the library and information science community is directed towards how people can most effectively search for and retrieve the information required to do their jobs. Although information retrieval is a key concern for recordkeepers, we have to be careful to ensure that the scope of our interest and endeavours remains focused on information as evidence, and not try to encompass the 'information for knowledge and awareness' purpose that is the function of librarians (see Oliver, 2017 and Nicholls, 2018 for discussion of the unique features of records literacy). However, it is important to work collaboratively with other information professionals, and including recordkeeping training goals in organisation-wide programmes will help to affirm the legitimacy of these goals. This is further discussed in the sections on assessment techniques and interventions below.

By taking this broader view of information literacy requirements we can find ways of delivering recordkeeping related training so that it is obviously relevant to the work that people are carrying out. If the need for recordkeeping is not generally recognised or understood in your organisation (as discussed in Chapter 2), then establishing this relevance is a key challenge in order for training to be successful. One way of doing this is to incorporate recordkeeping requirements as a key strategy for dealing with information overload.

Information overload

The ever-increasing quantity of information that is being created, coupled with multiple ICT channels (smartphones, tablets, personal computers), leads to people being quite simply overwhelmed. It becomes more and more difficult to segment the workplace from the home; consequently, the problems of information overload have been reported to result in significant stress and anxiety (Brey, 2012). While information overload has been an area of concern for library and information science (for a detailed literature review, see Bawden and Robinson, 2009), it has not attracted much serious attention from the recordkeeping community.

Information overload is not a new phenomenon but, as Brey notes, its dimensions have changed as technologies (particularly mobile computing) have developed, and these dimensions now include a feature that Brey characterises as 'message overload' (2012, xxiii). This message overload – for example, relentless e-mails demanding our attention – can be of key importance and interest to records managers. By developing and providing training for records management skills that can demonstrably assist in dealing with information overload, the benefits to users will be clear. See the section on interventions for a simple example to illustrate how this approach can be taken.

The boundaries between information literacy and digital literacy are very blurred, and often the terms are used interchangeably. The more our lives are dominated by ICTs, the more understandable this blurring becomes, by virtue of the fact that most of the information we are dealing with is digital. Here our use of 'digital literacy' refers to the needs of employees to understand how to work efficiently and effectively with digital information, ranging from awareness of online behaviours to an understanding of the medium- and long-term risks associated with digital information.

Digital literacy

As with information literacy, much of the research that has taken place and many of the resources that have been developed are directed towards students, whether at school or in higher education. However, there is also a lot of interest in workplace digital literacy – not surprisingly, given the pervasiveness of information technologies in the current business environment. A bewildering number of terms are used which encompass digital literacy, including ICT literacy, digital citizenship and so on. Concerns relating to digital literacy are not new, but have steadily gained more attention over the years.

At the end of the 20th century Rob Kling of Indiana University discussed the problem of assuming that expanded technological capabilities would be sufficient to enable internet access for all, and argued for the need to consider social access too:

> *social access* refers to know-how – a mix of professional knowledge, economic resources, and technical skills – for using technologies in ways that enhance professional practices and social life.
>
> (Kling, 2000, 226)

He goes on to describe the problems which home users were encountering in trying to use their new computers and access the internet, and suggests that, despite the decreasing cost of technology, the digital divide is actually increasing. The types of problems he describes are vividly familiar to those of us who were struggling with home computer use at that time, but probably incomprehensible to those now accustomed to using touch-screen interfaces and wireless internet connections.

There is no doubt that tremendous progress has been made in terms of usability and improving the human–computer interface, and this area will continue to be of key interest to technology developers and system designers. However, it is important to realise that seeming ease and fluency of use of technology can in fact mask significant underlying issues. These issues will include a lack of understanding of the fundamentals of how ICT systems work, how algorithms function and who governs the internet. This may result not only in completely unrealistic expectations but also an inability to evaluate whether or not outcomes are appropriate; for instance, using Google to search for information, while not being aware of the sophistication of the algorithms applied to rank results but simply accepting the first screen as the 'most relevant' resources.

It is much more difficult today to evaluate the extent of a person's digital literacy – the phrase which is now widely used to encompass Rob Kling's 'social access'. Evaluation is difficult because it is more likely that people will *appear* to be familiar with the use of information technology, than was the case 10 or 15 years earlier. People may appear to use technology with ease, checking e-mails and using apps on their mobile devices. However, knowing about file formats, or understanding why it matters where and how digital information is stored, is another issue entirely.

If identifying the problem is more difficult today, the same can also be said of working out how to tackle it. If someone thinks of themselves as a power user, as being extremely competent in using their technological tool or gadget, it's a very difficult thing to communicate that they are not actually as clever as they think they are. The phrase 'digital literacy' in itself may not be well received. Who wants to be told they are digitally illiterate?

This is a significant challenge, and tackling it involves tact and diplomacy, and the ability to empathise. Consequently, spending sufficient time to tailor the whole approach to assessment and subsequent training to your particular user group will be an investment that will pay off in the long term. Two aspects of digital literacy that can provide very effective approaches to records management-related training are described below: online behaviour and digital longevity.

Online behaviour

In the first edition of this book we introduced this section by emphasising the problematic nature of interacting online and the potential for personal musings and indiscretions to be globally visible. Those problems now seem comparatively benign, in the context of increasing online hate speech. The rise of social media usage and the use and misuse of channels such as Facebook and Twitter have dramatically signalled the need for digital literacy skills to navigate the online environment.

As mentioned in Chapter 1, in order to reintroduce forgetting in spite of the possibilities of technological infinite remembering, Mayer-Schönberger suggests a behavioural approach: digital abstinence.

Although individuals will vary enormously in the extent to which they are willing to participate in online communities, and the nature of that participation, the pervasiveness of online life means that most of us will leave substantial traces, knowingly or not. So digital abstinence is certainly not a feasible solution – especially today, when protecting our privacy on the web does not seem to be on the agenda of the most powerful nations in the world – and would necessitate turning the clock back. However, awareness of the consequences of online activities is a necessary and significant digital literacy skill.

As we noted in Chapter 1, the use of social media by organisations is rapidly increasing and has major implications for successful records management. Developing a training session on the perils and pitfalls of online behaviour will provide an effective means of introducing the fundamentals of recordkeeping in relation to using social media tools in the context of business activities. By framing key concepts in ways which will be appreciated and understood, we can demonstrate the relevance of recordkeeping concerns to information that is created using non-traditional media and channels.

Digital longevity

Digital preservation, digital continuity, digital longevity – all these phrases signify increasing attention being paid to making sure that digital information can be accessed in the future. This is a key concern if records management is to be viable in a digital environment, where we are very dependent on user behaviour. The use of new tools such as social media represents one opportunity for training, but we also need to focus on the much more routine information-creating activities that people probably now largely take for granted.

The greater the understanding of the nature of digital information and the ICT systems that are being used, the better the chances are that the inherent risks will be appreciated. Risk management may be a powerful notion to use in relation to any digital literacy training, particularly if the corporate culture emphasises risk awareness.

What's needed is an awareness of what happens after data has been input or read, encouraging people to think beyond the immediate create and capture dimensions. To achieve this goal it will be necessary to ensure that there is a basic understanding of the following three factors:

- the main characteristics of software development, including differentiation between open source and proprietary products
- file formats, including simple and complex documents
- storage systems, including networks, back-ups, portable storage devices and cloud computing.

Each of these factors needs to be considered in the context of time, and the consequences associated with the choices made in three, five and ten years' time – and longer. This is an area where we can use the blurring of home and work boundaries to our advantage, particularly if there is a low value assigned to records. The enormity of the risks associated with the very temporal nature of digital information can be effectively communicated with reference to people's personal digital memories. A desire to make sure that subsequent generations can retrieve and view digital photographs can be a very powerful motivation to learn.

Developing recordkeeping training in a way that makes it clear that the resulting skills can be applied in personal life as well as at work will be an effective way of communicating in those organisations where records are poorly understood and valued. The key characteristics of records as set out in ISO15489 – authenticity, reliability, integrity and usability – can all be incorporated into digital literacy training. Metadata can be introduced painlessly by developing examples of the type required to ensure these characteristics both at home and at work. An example to illustrate how this can be achieved is included in the section on next steps.

Assessment techniques

Given the importance of information literacy and digital literacy to today's workforce, the ideal approach to assessment is a holistic one, encompassing not just the recordkeeping perspective. Before you embark on any assessment activity it will therefore be essential to find out if any organisational training needs assessment has already been undertaken, so talk to the human resources and IT departments. The Computer Driving Licence skills programme is available both in Europe and further afield (ECDL Foundation, 2013), and if this certification programme is or has been followed, then there will be important baseline information that you will need to know about.

In order to develop records management training that fulfils the requirements of ISO15489 you will need to frame it in the context of information literacy and digital literacy priorities, rather than determining precisely what individual employees' skill sets consist of. If your organisation has embarked on a more comprehensive approach to assessing training needs, then it is critical to be a part of this. If not, then make sure that the key people in management know what you are doing, but proceed with your own assessment of training needs. The following suggestions are formulated under the assumption that training needs assessment is a solely records management-focused undertaking.

Desk research

The desk research component of this assessment consists of determining what the records management-specific training requirements are; that is, to identify what knowledge, skills and expertise the records management operation requires of its users. Further detail on this may emerge when the focus is on the second level two factor, environmental requirements (see Chapter 6). But it is important not to lose sight of the big-picture reasons that underpin the rationale for specific policies and procedures, such as an understanding of what records are and why they are important *for your organisation*.

System-specific training requirements must also be clarified at this stage. The skills that users need in an EDRMS that has been implemented are quite different to those that are needed in a shared-drive environment, and it is important to tailor training appropriately.

Identifying approaches to training

The key to assessment for information and digital literacy skills is to find out what information-related activities are of most concern to people. Rather than taking a traditional assessment approach and asking 'can you do x, y or z', you will be taking a more indirect route, and developing questions for use in a survey or interview format.

Survey questions

See Chapter 2 for general comments relating to survey design. You could combine questions that will provide insight into information-related competencies with any level one survey activity undertaken, or construct a very brief standalone questionnaire. The questions should aim to find out what concerns people have relating to working with information. For instance:

- Constant e-mail causes me stress: True/False/Don't Know
- Mobile devices mean I can't escape work information: Always/Often/Sometimes/Never/Not Applicable
- I find it difficult to find documents I have created over a year ago: Always/Often/Sometimes/Never/Not Applicable

It will also be important to provide an opportunity for people to identify additional concerns, so include an optional question to ensure that you are aware of any other issues that may be a source of anxiety. For instance:

- Please use this space to identify any other particular problems you encounter in working with information.

Interview questions

As explained in Chapter 2, interview questions should be formulated to encourage discussion. For instance:

- How do you cope with the demands of e-mail?
- Do you think that mobile devices make it easier to cope with work requirements?
- What are the main challenges you encounter in working with information?

The outcome from this needs assessment activity will enable you to develop training which can be directly framed to fit the specific concerns of employees.

Interventions

Bearing in mind the aims of our recordkeeping informatics standpoint, as explained in Chapter 1, seeing recordkeeping goals as one component in addressing the spectrum of information and digital literacy requirements is something to be aspired to. Recordkeeping informatics encourages records managers to work collaboratively with other information professionals within the organisation, and determining information and digital literacy training needs certainly provides an ideal opportunity for doing just that. The information-related competencies of employees should be a key concern across the organisation. If this has not been yet recognised by management and/or colleagues in IT or the library, this offers a perfect opportunity to show leadership. The first thing to do therefore is to find out if any work has already been undertaken, or if concerns have been raised in other sections of the organisation. Investigating this should help you to identify the key individuals to involve. If work has already been undertaken, build on it; if it has not, then at least you know who needs to be consulted in developing your components.

The key information you need to find out concerning information-related competencies can be summarised as follows:

- What are the key difficulties faced by employees in everyday information management?
- What understanding do they have of the technology and tools that they are required to use?

Developing training to address these needs should focus first on developing the underpinning information and digital literacy skills, before tackling system-specific training needs. The following two examples show how records management content can be framed in approaches that may resonate with users.

Presenting content from information literacy/digital literacy perspectives

1 Focus on a particular record type or genre, as this is likely to best reflect how people think about records. E-mail is a prime example. By focusing training specifically on e-mail management (e.g. giving guidance as to choice of actions depending on the role [primary or copied] of the recipient) it can be presented as a way of managing information overload while at the same time providing training in records management processes.
2 Take advantage of the blurring of work and home in the digital environment to develop clearly transferable skills which are

underpinned by records management concepts. For example, use a digital photo showing individuals, or better still, ask your trainees to bring along family photos. The photo (Figure 5.1) becomes a way of demonstrating the importance of contextual knowledge. Ask the following questions:

- Who is this man?
- Where is he? What is he doing?
- When was the photograph taken?
- Who took the photograph?
- Will future generations be able to see this photograph and understand their relationship to this person?

Discussing ways to answer these questions will enable you to highlight the key elements of metadata needed in order to provide sufficient context to explain the image, and to link them to the key characteristics of records.

Figure 5.1 *Example photograph for information literacy training*

The underlying principle is to develop training modules that are obviously practical and useful for your users; that is, make sure that the purpose and objectives will be perceived as being relevant and helpful. Users are much more likely to respond positively to a training module which offers skills in dealing with a particular record type (e.g. e-mail) in a particular, familiar context (e.g. e-mail management in our department), or with a specific record instantiation (e.g. the picture shown above), rather than a generic 'what is a record and why is it important' offering. Delivering training in recordkeeping concepts that will result in skills that can be applied in personal life will be a significant achievement, and will counteract the negative consequences of low or partial understanding of the value of organisational records and recordkeeping.

Summary and conclusions

A broader information literacy/digital literacy perspective on the knowledge, skills and expertise required by employees to fulfil their records management responsibilities means taking a radically different approach to training. The key to success is to understand the pressures and demands on users, and to use these as opportunities to get your message across. This chapter has identified three possible approaches, summarised in Table 5.1, which can be used as vehicles for recordkeeping training objectives.

Table 5.1 *Recordkeeping training objectives from the perspectives of information and digital literacy*

Approach/topic	Records management training objectives
Information overload	• Application of records management processes and controls
Online behaviour	• Understanding the ubiquitous nature of records • Awareness of records in multiplicity of media and formats
Digital longevity	• Awareness of key characteristics of records and associated risks • Understanding of metadata

The actual approaches/topics used will be identified as an outcome from assessment; the three suggested here are examples of likely candidates.

One important consideration that has not been addressed in this chapter is how training should be delivered – face to face, one on one, small group, written manuals, online – the choices are many and various. The decisions you make will be influenced by the information preferences of your users, as discussed in Chapter 3. The advantages and disadvantages of each option, and linkages to specific information preferences, are set out in the section on interventions in the next chapter.

References

Bawden, D. and Robinson, L. (2009) The Dark Side of Information: overload, anxiety and other paradoxes and pathologies, *Journal of Information Science*, **35**, 180–91.

Brey, P. (2012) Foreward. In Strother, J. B., Ulijn, J. M. and Fazal, Z. (eds), *Information Overload: an international challenge for professional engineers and technical communicators*, Wiley, xxi–xxv.

ECDL Foundation (2013) *About Us*, www.ecdl.org/index.jsp?p=93&n=94 [accessed 4 January 2013].

International Organization for Standardization (ISO) (2016) ISO15489- 1:2016 Information and documentation – Records management. Part 1: Concepts and principles.

Kling, R. (2000) Learning About Information Technologies and Social Change: the contribution of social informatics, *The Information Society*, **16**, 217–32.

Lloyd, A. (2011) Trapped Between a Rock and a Hard Place: what counts as information literacy in the workplace and how is it conceptualized? *Library Trends*, **60** (2), 277–96.

Mayer-Schönberger, V. (2009) *Delete: the virtue of forgetting in the digital age*, Princeton University Press.

Nicholls, C. V. (2018) Making the Case for Recordkeeping Literacy: a narrative approach, *Archives and Manuscripts*, **46** (2), 143–57.

Oliver, G. (2017) The Records Perspective: a neglected aspect of information literacy, *Information Research*, **22** (1).

Savolainen, R. (2002) Network Competence and Information Seeking on the Internet: from definitions towards a social cognitive model, *Journal of Documentation*, **58** (2), 211–26.

Widén, G. and Karim, M. (2018) Role of Information Culture in Workplace Information Literacy: a literature review. In: Kurbanoğlu, S., Boustany, J., Špiranec, S., Grassian, E., Mizrachi, D. and Roy, L. (eds,) *Information Literacy in the Workplace*. ECIL 2017. Communications in Computer and Information Science, vol 810, Springer, Cham.

CHAPTER 6

Awareness of environmental requirements relating to records

This is the second of the two chapters focusing on factors at level two of the ICF, and addresses the extent to which staff are aware of environmental requirements relating to records and recordkeeping, and the need to develop training that focuses on this area.

The phrase *environmental requirements* is used as an umbrella term to encompass the laws, standards and norms present in the broader societal, jurisdictional and organisational context. They include regional, national and provincial or local legislation, as well as standards and codes of practice. Clearly, the first step in addressing this aspect of information culture is to identify what is relevant to a specific organisation. This is discussed in the first part of the chapter. This is followed by the steps needed to find out if existing organisational policy reflects those requirements, and to identify and take action on any gaps. The final stage is to find out to what extent employees are familiar with requirements and, most importantly, whether they are able (and willing) to put these requirements into practice. This assessment stage may involve surveying users – in contrast to the first two investigative stages, which can largely be explored by researching existing databases. Sample survey questions that can be used to identify training needs are suggested. The final part of the chapter discusses the training-related delivery choices that have to be made, and includes consideration of the relative advantages and disadvantages of different training-delivery modes (for example, group versus one on one, synchronous versus asynchronous) and highlights the need to develop sustainable training programmes.

It is important at this point to recall the 'soft' perspective that underlies our approach. Understanding the environment in which recordkeeping activities take place does not simply mean identifying external and internal requirements based on the available formal documentation. The latter will not tell us how the organisation actually works, how it enacts any of the identified requirements, how such requirements influence people's behaviour. Managing records is a social phenomenon that takes place in 'human activity systems' (Checkland, 1999), which are inevitably messy and unpredictable because they involve us, human beings who may always choose to act otherwise. While in the controlled environment of a laboratory 'hard' science researchers can exactly define and manipulate their variables; in real-world situations we should always be aware that the way people interpret and apply existing laws, regulations and policies may be very different from the way that they are spelled out in official documents.

Compliance is an important word in the recordkeeping vocabulary. However, there is nothing objective or unquestionable about it. Interpreting laws, regulations and standards, and understanding if and how they fit with existing organisational policies and practices and how they could be applied to specific contexts are subjective acts that precede and shape compliance. One of the goals of this chapter is to shed light on the continuous interplay between environmental and recordkeeping requirements. Such requirements both constrain and enable information practices in ways that reflect the cultural characteristics of the social groups that created them.

Researching recordkeeping requirements

As we emphasise throughout this book, our discussion of information culture is embedded in one key 'environmental requirement': the International Organisation for Standardisation's (ISO) International Standard on Records Management, ISO15489. There is no better place to start thinking about the environmental requirements for recordkeeping that apply to your organisation than by checking to see exactly what the records management standard has to say.

The standard provides very clear direction that the methodology for the design and implementation of records systems must include the identification of *requirements for records*:

> Records requirements are based on an analysis of business activity and its context …, and are derived from the following:
>
> a) business needs;
> b) legal and regulatory requirements;
> c) community or societal expectations.

> (ISO15489-1, 7.4 c)

This part of the standard shows the influence of the Australian DIRKS methodology. In Chapter 1 we introduced DIRKS, and discussed its relationship to our ICF approach (see pp. 23–5). Because there is significant overlap with the DIRKS approach, DIRKS documentation could be a useful source of guidance for researching recordkeeping requirements. Step A Preliminary Investigation and Step C Identification of Recordkeeping Requirements are the most relevant sections of DIRKS, particularly if you need to know about the Australian context or, more specifically, the State of New South Wales, as this is where most of the examples are drawn from (DIRKS Manual, 2007).

Legislation

ISO15489 is unequivocal about the need to identify which legislation is relevant to recordkeeping in the organisation, in order to help to identify the requirements for records to be created and captured. It also reminds us that attention has to be paid to the specific industry or sector within which the organisation or community operates.

Advice aimed at an international audience has to be as generic as possible. The specific legislation that applies, and the provisions of that legislation, will vary according to the jurisdiction. Jurisdiction is a useful term, which for our purposes can be interpreted as referring to a set of laws applicable to a particular area. The area in question could be a country, or other government entity such as a state or province. If recordkeeping in your organisation or community has international dimensions, then it will be important to take into account all possible jurisdictions involved in business activities.

Locating relevant legislation

The rapid spread of electronic communications and the emergence of a new, more transparent way of conceiving citizen–state relationships have caused radical changes in society, which, in many countries, have manifested in a considerable increase in the legislation dedicated to various aspects of the 'information society'. In Italy, for instance, following the modernisation of public administration and the 'dematerialisation' of documentary evidence through the introduction of ICT in the workplace, dozens of new laws, directives and technical rules have been issued at the national level since the early 1990s, forming a rather incoherent regulatory constellation. To help practitioners orient themselves in such a 'legislative jungle', interest groups and professional associations (e.g. the National Association of Italian

Archivists [ANAI]) have created accessible databases of current norms and offer guidance through online discussion fora and listserves.[1]

Elizabeth Shepherd and Geoffrey Yeo provide suggestions for up-to-date online resources for the major English-speaking countries,[2] pointing out that outside North America it is generally much better to rely on sources compiled for the legal profession rather than on those compiled for records managers, as the former are more likely to be kept up to date (Shepherd and Yeo, 2003, 40–1). A general piece of advice is not to rely on any published source listing legal requirements that is not updated as necessary. Subscription CD-Roms are available through ARMA International, containing legal retention requirements relating to the USA and Canada. Subscription resources can be very costly, so the funding you have available will govern the choices you make here.

Understanding the legislation

Finding the relevant legislation is one thing, but making sense of it is another matter entirely. Further very practical guidance that will help greatly in making sense of the complexity of legislation is provided in Guideline 2 of the PARBICA toolkit (PARBICA, 2009). Once again, the antecedents and influences can be traced to DIRKS and ISO15489, the difference here being in the clarity of the guidance provided.

The toolkit was developed by the Pacific Regional Branch of the International Council on Archives as a very pragmatic resource for use by practitioners working in a region with no formal educational programme for records or archives management. However, this should not be taken to mean that the guidance is overly simplistic or not relevant to other regions. In particular, Guideline 2: Identifying Recordkeeping Requirements is a very well-written and useful source of advice that can be easily applied to quite different contexts.

This guideline distinguishes between enabling legislation (a law that legally creates a given organisation), administered legislation (laws that the organisation has oversight of) and administrative legislation (laws which may apply to many or all organisations in particular sectors, such as freedom of information, financial transactions or archives acts). Regulations – rules that can be developed by organisations with the requisite authority relating to a particular law – are also identified as a separate category or class to be investigated (PARBICA, 2009, 7–8). Categorising legislation in this way helps to provide a preliminary framework for research and will assist in making sure that attention is paid to all areas.

After identifying relevant legislation Guideline 2 provides a practical approach to investigating each instrument to determine whether or not it includes any recordkeeping requirements. The types of requirement are categorised as below, together with helpful examples phrased in 'legalese':

- create a record – for example, 'There shall be a register of licenses'
- include certain information in a record – for example, 'The form must include the applicant's name and date of birth'
- create a record in a certain form – for example, 'Applications must be lodged using an official form'
- keep a record for a certain amount of time – for example, 'The Registrar must keep all approved applications for a period of seven years from the date of their lodgement'
- destroy a record after a certain amount of time – for example, 'The Registrar must destroy all unsuccessful applications one year after the date of their lodgement'
- provide access to a record – for example, 'The Register must be open for inspection by the public'
- prevent access to a record – for example, 'Applications must be stored in such a way as to keep their contents private'.

(PARBICA, 2009, 11)

Of course, it will be critical for individual members of staff to be aware of any specific legislative responsibilities relating to any one of the above points, particularly in organisations with flat structures without a centralised command-and-control type of records management system. This awareness is the crux of this chapter, and will be considered below in the section on assessment techniques.

Other requirements

PARBICA Guideline 2 also identifies the need to investigate a much more difficult-to-define source of information for possible recordkeeping requirements: external reviews of the organisation and the way it does its work, such as audit reports (PARBICA, 2009, 9).

To this list of potential sources for recordkeeping requirements we can add standards and codes of practice. The ISO9000 series, for instance, includes references to requirements for records to be created and maintained in order to provide evidence of quality processes having been followed. Another example comes from the health sector in New Zealand, which has a specific code of practice relating to the retention and storage of health information. These requirements set out some fundamental guidelines for recordkeeping in any organisation that is active in the health sector, ranging from District Health Boards to general practitioners.

How to do it

The foregoing discussion has hopefully made it very clear that researching recordkeeping requirements is a very fundamental component of establishing a records management programme. It is not surprising therefore that this need is reflected in standards and guidance developed by archival authorities and professional associations. However, this wealth of information can seem daunting, so some general observations will be made here about how to get started.

Practitioners can approach this research exercise in a number of different ways. The traditional, best-practice approach would be to begin by systematically searching online databases (depending on the jurisdiction, these may be freely accessible via the internet or may require a subscription via a specialist law library) for relevant legislation, using the categories identified in the PARBICA guideline (enabling, administered and administrative) as a starting point.

However, if you don't have previous experience with this type of database you can very easily get lost in the detail and, depending on the size and complexity of your organisation, the process could be very inefficient and take a great deal of time. For this reason we suggest that you start by asking colleagues in the organisation, rather than with the formal databases. Auditors, accountants, legal practitioners – any or all would be a good first port of call. However, don't ask specifically about recordkeeping require-ments: just which legislation is applicable (if recordkeeping requirements are known about and mentioned, so much the better, but this will not always be the case).

Starting by asking key staff members about relevant legislation will provide you with a quick and easy start to your research. Undertaking the formal search would then be the second step, and would be much more focused, as you would be trying to spot additional laws rather than starting from scratch.

Organisational or community policy

After finding out what the external requirements are (in DIRKS and ISO15489 terminology, the recordkeeping requirements), the next stage is to find out whether or not these requirements are reflected in your organisation's internal policy. For instance, if your jurisdiction has legislation relating to the protection of personal information, has your organisation or community issued a policy that accurately reflects the relevant provisions? Finding this out may be a straightforward task, involving checking recordkeeping policy against the external requirements. However, if your organisation or community is particularly large and complex or loosely structured, then the checking process becomes much more involved. For example, in a university there is likely to be policy relating to information about students that may have been developed by the student administration division, possibly without recourse to or input from the recordkeeping function.

Lateral thinking will be required to identify where likely policy may have been developed. Talking to key stakeholders (e.g. the audit team) will assist. In very large entities this may feel like hunting for the needle in the haystack, but it will not be wasted effort. The more understanding you have of the way that your organisation or community works, the better the chances of recordkeeping programme goals and objectives succeeding.

After the comparison between applicable external requirements and internal policy, or 'gap analysis', has been carried out, it will be necessary to amend your policy and its related procedures as required. It is only once internal policy is up to date and accurately reflects the relevant legislation and standards of the external environment that we can turn our attention to making sure that all employees or community members are familiar with, and understand, their responsibilities with respect to recordkeeping.

Assessment techniques

This chapter is quite different from previous chapters in that the preceding discussion of the context (environmental requirements) has focused on analysis and investigation. It may seem a little strange to now move into consideration of assessment techniques, but this is because it is only after establishing the current situation with respect to environmental requirements that we can shift our attention to our ICF level two factor. To reiterate, this is the knowledge that people have about organisational or community requirements to create and maintain records, or the extent to which people are aware of their responsibilities with respect to recordkeeping.

This is by default the focus of traditional approaches to records management training. Following the ISO15489 guidance that training must be provided, the obvious approach has been to focus on delivering training on what recordkeeping policies say, and what procedures have to be followed. By approaching this topic from the perspective of establishing clarity as to what societal requirements exist, and then ensuring that they are reflected in internal policy, we are endeavouring to make sure that there is consistency between what may be regarded as separate elements in setting up a recordkeeping programme. Our approach is less prescriptive than the traditional one, allowing for adjustment of the rules when they do not correspond to people's behaviour and values. Furthermore, approaching policy- and procedure-specific training as an output directly related to requirements identification will ensure that recordkeepers will be supported by a strong rationale and justification for their activities.

In Chapter 5 the approach to determining training needs was non-traditional, in that the focus was on finding out what information-related activities were of most concern, rather than whether people knew how to do something. However, we can take a much more direct and conventional approach to determining training needs in relation to awareness of environmental requirements. Appropriate questions can be developed for use in a survey or interview format, if necessary. This is an important proviso, as this level two area is unique in that you may already have a very good grasp of the situation. If the recordkeeping function is relatively new and policies and procedures have only recently been developed, then you will know that you are working from a blank slate, and can be confident that specific training in recordkeeping requirements is needed by all. However, if the recordkeeping programme is an established part of the organisation and training has been given in the past, then this needs-assessment exercise will be necessary.

Survey questions

General comments about survey design are provided in Chapter 2. For this assessment, either you can develop questions to gauge people's awareness of recordkeeping requirements in conjunction with other assessment activity, or you can develop a very brief standalone questionnaire. The focus of the questions will vary according to the requirements that apply to your particular setting, but the following examples can be used as templates:

- I fully understand what information needs to be protected according to the Privacy Act: Always/Most of the time/Sometimes/Never/Not Applicable
- I know how to respond to a request made under the Freedom of Information Act: Always/Most of the time/Sometimes/Never/Not Applicable

Incidentally, the 'not applicable' option may be very telling, if, for instance, all employees deal with personal information. It is also important to include an opportunity for employees to nominate areas that they are unclear about:

- Please use this space to identify any legislation, standards or organisational policy relating to managing information where you are unclear about your responsibilities.

Interviews

If you are conducting individual or focus group interviews, training needs can be explored by using questions which are much more open and which will provide opportunities for following up:

- How do you go about responding to a request made under the Freedom of Information Act?
- When and why would you consult our recordkeeping policy?

Interventions

Up to now our focus in this and the preceding chapter has been on the content of the training that is needed. The approach that you take to the content will be influenced by the values accorded to records, as discussed in Chapter 2. Just as important are the decisions you will need to make about delivery, the 'how' of the training programme. In any organisation or community you will encounter a range of different learning styles, so remember that you cannot assume that everyone learns in the same way. An advantage of the ICF is that the insight gleaned at level one about information preferences can be used to take into account these different responses to the ways in which information is communicated. As explained in Chapter 3, variations in high- and low-context communication and in attitudes to time are key considerations to factor into the overall planning of a training programme.

The choices to be made will include decisions about whether to train in groups or one to one, when training should be delivered, how the content should be presented, planning for ongoing training and to what extent training should be mandatory.

Training should also be an opportunity for the trainer to learn about shared perceptions, workarounds and views of the organisational reality that individuals and groups may have. This knowledge is often unexpressed, and making it emerge should be one of the objectives of the training activity.

Based on it, the trainer might adjust his or her message and may eventually suggest changes to existing policies and procedures in order to reflect employees' preferences and needs.

Group or individual training

The first question to consider is whether or not to conduct training on a group basis. If so, how should the groups be constituted? Should they be composed of people working in the same functional area, or consist of people at the same level of the hierarchy? For example, everyone from the most senior to most junior in the finance department, or the executive management team spanning the whole organisation. Decisions will be influenced by cultural considerations. For instance, if organisational employees are likely to hold collectivist values, training by workgroup is likely to be most appropriate. If there is high respect for power distance, training groups consisting of members at all levels of the hierarchy may not be successful if there is a risk of loss of face. The pressures and demands of daily work will also need to be taken into account. Will a training session that takes people out of their regular working environment be regarded as a welcome break from routine, or a further burden impacting on their ability to meet organisational targets?

Training targeted at groups can be conducted either in real time (synchronously) or more flexibly, not requiring the presence of everyone at the same time, in the same place (asynchronously). There are distinct advantages and disadvantages to each, and choices involve taking cultural characteristics into account. Synchronous training means that time has to be set aside for the specific purpose of learning, so that it is not competing with other priorities and other distractions. Of course, this can mean that it is resented, in which case there is likely to be considerable resistance to taking part. It would require a lot of skill on the part of the trainer to successfully achieve learning objectives in this setting.

Asynchronous training (using self-study online and/or print-based materials) provides much more flexibility: people can choose where and when to take part, thus having control over fitting it into their working day. However, by its very nature it requires a high degree of motivation on the part of the individual learners; and the more choice there is of whether or not to do something, the less likely it may be to happen. To compensate, a lot of attention must be paid to the attractiveness of the course materials, usability features and the use of techniques to encourage participation, such as acknowledging completion of tasks. Asynchronous training is a very worthwhile option, but should not be regarded as an easy or less costly choice.

If training is not conducted on a group basis, then due consideration needs to be given as to how best one-on-one training should be delivered. Options will include working with people individually, in a coaching role, or providing self-study materials, either online or in print. Once again, the choice is between synchronous and asynchronous delivery, and the comments made about these modes with respect to groups also apply here.

In Chapter 3 we noted that preferences for asynchronous as opposed to synchronous communication have been suggested to be linked to different national cultural characteristics. According to the Hall communication model, collectivist cultures are more likely to prefer synchronous communication, individualist cultures are more likely to prefer asynchronous (Hall and Hall, 1989), so this is something to bear in mind. Above all, do not assume that everyone will respond in the same way, and be prepared to cater for a variety of preferences in order to try to minimise the number of reluctant and unwilling participants.

Training materials

Whether training is delivered on a group or individual basis, there should be some sort of documentation provided. This may constitute the training itself (e.g. self-paced workbook or online resource) or may be handouts of some kind, such as a take-away reminder of key points. Regardless of where the documentation fits on this scale, due attention must be paid to catering for those high-context and low-context communication differences as discussed in Chapter 3. People from cultures characterised as high-context or collectivist may find pictures and images more effective than text, and vice versa for people from low-context or individualist countries. These are very sweeping statements, but should serve as an important reminder that all people simply do not learn in the same way. A picture may well be worth a thousand words to some – but not to others.

The use of online rather than print materials will be greatly influenced by the resources you have at your disposal. Developing online resources from the ground up involves a lot of specialist expertise; using pre-packaged, generic online courses may be problematic because records management is so context specific. However, online resources may have the potential for greater interactivity between trainer and trainees, and allow for more flexibility, as the content as well as the delivery mode can be adjusted as the need arises. Another advantage of relying on online training is that information about the learning process may be easily obtained in the form of usage statistics. And, most importantly, you may increase the appeal and effectiveness of your training measure by including audio/visual animations, videos or other dynamic features in your materials.

The trainer

Deciding who should conduct the training is an important consideration. If resourcing permits, contracting an external person to deliver it may seem an attractive option. But give careful thought to the ramifications of this decision. Might it be taken to imply that the records manager and their team do not have the knowledge and skills required? Will the external trainer have sufficient knowledge of your organisational context, including the personalities involved, to be effective? Workplace training is not easy; if trainees feel patronised, then the desired outcomes will not be achieved. On the other hand, bringing someone in from outside may be seen as the only effective way of communicating, so your knowledge and understanding of your users will be paramount in making this decision. Using a 'train the trainer' approach (for instance, designating power users of recordkeeping systems for each work unit) may also be a very valid strategy to ensure that training continues (for comments about sustainable training see p. 107).

Planning a programme

Training is hard work. So much effort has to go into planning and delivering training sessions that it can be very tempting to simply stop after initial objectives (e.g. to provide training to all employees on x, y or z) have been accomplished. In order to derive ongoing benefit from all the effort expended it will be necessary to take a much longer-term and more holistic view. Decisions will need to be made as to what happens after an initial round of training, what follow-up sessions need to happen and how the needs of new employees should be met. If there is an organisation-wide orientation programme for new staff members, should records management training be a part of that, or would it be better to schedule recordkeeping training for later on, so as to maximise its impact?

Must it be compulsory?

Given the critical nature of training so that all employees will play their part in ensuring successful records management, there is no question that the need for training will be mandatory. This is another characteristic that may well alienate users and act as a demotivator, so we urge flexibility and sensitivity.

Take into account an individual's background and existing knowledge and skills, and be prepared to make exceptions. If training is going to be superfluous and cover very familiar ground, do not insist on it. Listening and deciding based on a particular set of circumstances will be much more respected than insistence on doing something 'because everyone must'.

Research on how people learn in the workplace teaches us that most organisational learning happens through socialisation and participation in work practices (see Lave and Wenger, 1991). If conducting formal training does not seem to be a good strategy, because of negative experiences in the past, unavailability of resources or any other reasons, we recommend the 'indirect approach'. For instance, records managers may offer their assistance to other employees in the organisation and work side by side for a while. This goes beyond what is usually known as 'floor walking', where experts provide on-site support to users sporadically and temporarily. It is really about 'community building', which may be achieved through inviting non-specialist records management staff to become active participants in (a limited number of) records-related operations by accepting to collaborate with records managers in their day-to-day work.

Sustainable training

The choices made about how best to deliver training will be strongly influenced by the resources (money and time) available. It may be necessary to develop a range of options to cater for the characteristics and learning styles of your users. Above all, training must be sustainable. Employees will come and go, community members may be very transient, so training content will change over time and the overall programme must be developed with this in mind. Establishing a programme that aims to train the trainer could be an effective and efficient way to proceed, but make sure that the designated trainers continue to receive support and encouragement. They should be regarded as very valuable assets, and be treated accordingly.

Finally, always remember to evaluate the training. It is essential to get feedback from trainees as to what worked and what did not, and vital to incorporate this feedback into the design of subsequent training sessions. Make sure that all training participants are given the opportunity to provide anonymous feedback. This can take the form of a simple questionnaire distributed at the end of the session, asking people to list up to three things that were effective and three things that were not, and to make any suggestions for improvement.

Summary and conclusions

This chapter has focused on the knowledge, skills and competencies of all users in relation to their recordkeeping responsibilities: the policies and procedures that are the traditional focus of recordkeeping training. Our starting point for the identification of training needs was a systematic identification of external requirements as represented by recordkeeping-related provisions in legislation and other rules, regulations and standards. The next stage was to ensure that these requirements are adequately and accurately reflected in internal policy. The recordkeeping requirements that fit your organisation or community will be the outcome of a balancing exercise between the abstract demands of applicable legislation and the concrete needs and expectations of your workplace. Only after these components have been addressed and any adaptations have been made can attention turn to identifying users' training needs.

Whether or not additional assessment activity is needed to determine the features of this level two factor in organisations or communities will depend on the maturity of the recordkeeping programme and the prevalence of good practice. If the relevant policies are newly developed and there is no history of training provision, it can be safely assumed that training needs to be developed for all. If the recordkeeping programme is well established and training has been provided in the past, some further investigative work will be necessary to ascertain what the specific training needs are.

The section on interventions identified the decisions that need to be made about training delivery. This discussion is also applicable to the information-related competencies training covered in Chapter 5. Key questions are whether to deliver training on a group or individual basis, synchronously or asynchronously, formally or informally, whether to use online or traditional print resources and who should do the training. It is essential to take the different information preferences into account, so the assessment activity described in Chapter 3 must be used to help shape a contextually appropriate training programme.

As ISO15489 makes clear, training is essential for staff at all levels of the organisation. But poorly planned and executed training which has not been designed in accordance with users' needs can be a negative experience and will not contribute to achieving the goals of the recordkeeping programme. Taking into account the pressures of the workplace on employees, or the reasons for engaging with a particular community, being sympathetic to competing demands and priorities will help you to make the right decisions. Training should be enjoyable and fun, a positive experience that will motivate and encourage.

Furthermore, training should be seen as an opportunity not only to teach about best practice but also to learn from training participants about their perhaps not-so-good practices. This knowledge of actual recordkeeping behaviour is essential so as to ensure that policies continue to be aligned with the recordkeeping culture of the workplace.

Notes

1   Italian norms relevant to records management and archives are available on the ANAI website at www.anai.org/anai-cms/cms.view?munu_str=0_1_2&numDoc=101 [accessed 24 January 2020].

2   Current URLs for Australia are www.austlii.edu.au and www.comlaw.gov.au, for Britain www.bailii.org, with the addition of New Zealand's http://legislation.govt.nz [accessed 9 January 13].

References

Checkland, P. (1999) *System Thinking, System Practice*, Wiley.

Hall, E. T. and Hall, M. R. (1989). *Understanding Cultural Differences,* Intercultural Press.

International Organization for Standardization (ISO) (2016) ISO15489-1:2016 Information and documentation – Records management. Part 1: Concepts and principles, 2nd edn.

Lave, J. and Wenger, E. (1991) *Situated Learning: legitimate peripheral participation,* Cambridge University Press.

PARBICA (2009) *Recordkeeping for Good Governance Toolkit. Guideline 2 Identifying recordkeeping requirements,* www.parbica.org/sharing/publications/recordkeeping-for-good-governance/guideline-02.aspx [accessed 18 September 2013].

Shepherd, E. and Yeo, G. (2003) *Managing Records: a handbook of principles and practice,* Facet Publishing.

State Records NSW (2007) *DIRKS Manual,* www.records.nsw.gov.au/recordkeeping/dirks-manual [accessed 10 January 2013].

PART 4

CHAPTER 7

Corporate information governance and recordkeeping systems and tools

This chapter considers the ICF at level three, the tip of the pyramid. Features at this level are open to change, but are most susceptible if they are approached with good understanding of the characteristics of the features at levels one and two.

Information governance is a very widely used phrase, so this chapter begins by discussing the concept in order to clearly differentiate our focus, which is specifically on the organisational information technology infrastructure and the recordkeeping systems and tools that this infrastructure supports. However, it is not possible to limit consideration to simply what is happening internally, because organisations rely increasingly on external services to carry out their operations. In particular, cloud computing cannot be ignored, as it has massive implications for recordkeeping. Security considerations, the need to manage the delicate balance between protecting records from unauthorised use while facilitating access, are discussed. Recordkeeping systems and tools are considered from the perspective that they need to be embedded in all systems. Assessment techniques are very practical and do not necessitate in-depth expertise in IT. Profiling provides an approach to reviewing corporate IT as reflected in the organisation's approach to information architecture. The coherence of the architecture can be identified by determining the extent to which the information systems in use interconnect. Key questions are: is the same data used by multiple systems? Is data re-entry required at any point? Are multiple logons required to accomplish related tasks?

Also relevant here are the organisation's IT policies and procedures, identifying any which may impact on employees' recordkeeping behaviours and perhaps motivate unauthorised workarounds. The section on interventions suggests practical tips for working collaboratively with IT departments.

Information governance

Given the ever-increasing capacities to create and store information, information governance is a hot topic for society in general, and has been widely seen by the recordkeeping profession as an opportunity to demonstrate its relevance. As discussed by Geoffrey Yeo in his 2018 book, *Records, Information and Data*, since the beginning of the 21st century the term 'information governance' has been promoted as 'a response, not just to the explosion of technology or to notions of an incipient Information Society, but also to the growth of what might be called the compliance agenda' (Yeo, 2018, 66). Organisational compliance with laws and regulations, with particular regard to the implementation of freedom of information and privacy legislation, records retention and disposition scheduling and the support of the organisation in cases of litigation, has always been one of the main objectives of records managers and a pillar of any recordkeeping policies and systems. So why not talk about 'records governance' instead? The UK's Information and Records Management Society (IRMS) explained their emphasis on 'information assets' as a key theme of their 2012 conference as follows:

> Information assets are part of the life-blood of an Organisation. In this age of information explosion, with more and more information gathered, stored and moved about, how we best keep our information assets secure and best utilise them in a timely, appropriate and lawful manner is both increasingly important and increasing complex to achieve.
>
> (IRMS, 2012)

Following suit, Australasia's professional records management association announced the theme of their 2013 convention as information governance, describing it as follows:

> a holistic approach to managing corporate information by implementing processes, roles, controls and metrics that treat information as a valuable business asset.

> The goal of a holistic approach to information governance is to make information assets available to those who need them, while streamlining management, reducing storage costs and ensuring compliance. This, in turn, allows the company to reduce the risks associated with unmanaged or inconsistently managed information and be more agile in response to a changing marketplace.
>
> (RIMPA, 2012)

Information governance has since then retained significant prominence. The 2020 call for papers for RIMPA (Records and Information Management Professionals Australasia) includes digital information management governance as a topic, under the theme of Digital Futurism and Leadership.[1]

Our professional discourse suggests that information governance could be viewed as a rebranding of records management. The two quotes above exemplify this tendency, particularly if the phrase 'information governance' were replaced with records management, and 'information assets' were replaced with 'records'. As is discussed in the next chapter, our domain is characterised by non-exclusive and often contested terminology, which can lead to ambivalent or even contradictory positions. Those positions can be poles apart – on the one hand insisting on a very specific and narrow focus on certain types and specific forms of information, while on the other seeming to claim responsibility for all organisational information. Both positions can be severely detrimental to our future in terms of being able to demonstrate the relevance of our specialised expertise. In the former case it is essential to have a sufficiently broad perspective and understanding of organisational activities in order to recognise that records are being created in a variety of different ways, not necessarily in designated recordkeeping systems. In the latter case it is essential to recognise the roles and responsibilities of our fellow information professionals such as librarians and data managers, and to understand the unique purpose of each endeavour. The recordkeeping informatics perspective described in Chapter 1 provides a way of recognising the complexity of the situation today. The key message to keep repeating is that it is essential to identify the distinctiveness of each approach within the broad information domain, but also to understand how to bring our strengths to bear in collaborative partnership with others. We will therefore continue to refer to information governance as a well-established, all-encompassing term, although our focus is on the special role played by recordkeeping, as a culturally dependent set of concepts and practices enacted by organisations and communities to ensure that whatever they consider to be evidence of their activities is created and preserved in ways that work for them.

Synergies between records management and information governance have been recognised, and in the USA a white paper was published setting out how the Information Governance Model complements ARMA International's Generally Accepted Recordkeeping Principles (GARP) (EDRM, 2011). Specific mention in this paper of decision rights and an accountability framework together with acknowledgement of the need to influence information-related behaviours sheds a more precise light on information governance, and starts to show the applicability of this concept to information culture. The white paper points back to ARMA's information governance maturity model, which was discussed in Chapter 1. As explained earlier, taking an information culture approach provides a clear point of departure from existing positivist survey instruments such as the maturity models, and enables a much more nuanced view of the various factors and influences in successful recordkeeping.

Europe's DLM (Document Lifecycle Management) Forum's discussion paper on information governance provides a useful description of information governance (DLM Forum, 2012). This document makes reference to the international standard definition for the corporate governance of information technology:

> the system by which the current and future use of IT is directed and controlled. Corporate governance of IT involves evaluating and directing the use of IT to support the organization and monitoring this use to achieve plans. It includes the strategy and policies for using IT within an organization.
>
> (ISO/IEC 38500:2008)

This very precise definition fits with our use of the governance concept in the ICF, as our focus is very much on the technology infrastructure used by organisations and how recordkeeping functions are embedded in it – whether through dedicated systems or through a more diffused approach. Of course, any consideration of organisational technological infrastructure is no longer restricted to in-house capabilities (see the section below on cloud computing for further discussion); but decisions regarding the extent to which cloud computing services will be used are made in-house, so this presents an opportunity to bring our influence to bear.

The origins of the governance concept can be seen in much earlier discussion by Thomas Davenport, in his depiction of information ecology (Davenport, 1997). The aims of taking an information ecology perspective are very similar to those proposed here to delineate information cultures, despite considerable difference in the detail. The common thread is an emphasis on a broad, holistic approach to information management in organisations. In previous work Gillian has used Davenport's models of political states (Davenport, 1997, 67–82) as a way to provide insight into the information technology manifestations of information governance (Oliver, 2008). These political states are described in detail below (see the section on assessment techniques).

To summarise, in our information culture approach, governance is referred to very specifically in the context of corporate IT infrastructure, with particular reference to the technologies that support recordkeeping. Factors at levels one and two in the ICF (respect for records, information sharing, training, for example) can easily be seen to be significant features in information governance in the more holistic sense, so it is important to be very precise about what is considered here at level three.

At level three, our focus is on the features of the technological infrastructure which have been established within the organisation to manage records. This is sometimes referred to under the banner of information architecture, and includes consideration of security and the use of cloud computing.

Information architecture

Information architecture as a concept and discipline has been applied to different environments, so, just as with information governance, it is essential to explain exactly what the focus is in a recordkeeping context. The term first began to be used in the early 1990s, in reference to information systems architecture within organisations. Brandt Allen and Andrew Boynton (1991) explain information architecture as follows:

> the set of policies and rules that govern an organization's actual and planned arrangements of computers, data, human resources, communication facilities, software, and management responsibilities. Information architecture has replaced organizational design, planning systems, and financial controls as the key to business design. Architecture specifies how and why the pieces fit together as they do, where they go, when they're needed, and why and how changes will be implemented.
>
> (Allen and Boynton, 1991, 435)

We do not propose that recordkeepers need to become experts in the finer details of information architecture. The technical detail can be overwhelming, but that should not present an insurmountable barrier. It will be much more useful to develop an overall sense of the characteristic features of the architecture, and for this reason we suggest the use of Davenport's typology of political states (see Assessment techniques, below).

Security

Consideration of security should without a doubt include the records professional's understanding of one of the key tensions associated with recordkeeping, namely, balancing the need to protect information from unauthorised access with facilitation of access and retrieval. If the balance is wrong, the records professional will be perceived either as a gatekeeper or, at the other extreme, as someone who causes scandal by revealing confidential information.

Ethical considerations relating to recordkeeping are extremely important. By the nature of their role, records professionals will have access to extremely confidential information relating to employees and the activities and goals of the organisation. Their position is one of trust, and their personal conduct has to demonstrate trustworthiness in every respect. This is discussed further in the next chapter, which considers trust and trustworthiness. But here our focus is on the processes and controls implemented to maintain the security of records and other information.

The international standard makes it clear that organisations need to have formal access and permissions rules which may apply to both internal and external users of the records (ISO15489-1, 8.4).

Attitudes to security are undoubtedly affected by cultural influences. Chapter 3 considered attitudes to information sharing, and these will influence the types of security regime that are established. Any restrictions on access to information within an organisation must be well thought out, defensible and culturally appropriate, otherwise non-compliance and even sabotage are likely to be the result.

Cloud computing

One area where records professionals really need to be proactive, and aware of the advantages and disadvantages, is cloud computing (Stuart and Bromage, 2010 provide an overview of the main issues from a recordkeeping perspective). There are undoubted benefits to organisations in outsourcing their information-processing requirements, including storage, to external providers. The standards world (in this case, the US National Institute of Standards and Technology) provides a definition of cloud computing which can be considered authoritative:

> a model for enabling ubiquitous, convenient, on-demand network access to a shared pool of configurable computing resources (e.g. networks, servers, storage, applications, and services) that can be rapidly provisioned and released with minimal management effort or service provider interaction.
>
> (Mell and Grance, 2011)

The inclusion of minimum service requirements in this definition acknowledges that cloud computing involves much more than simply outsourcing the storage of digital information. The speed and ease of response is of primary importance, so this definition at least provides a yardstick by which cloud computing services can be assessed.

However, the risks inherent in cloud computing are great, and are of particular concern to our mission to safeguard and manage information as evidence to document the accountability requirements of organisations. How can we be certain that information deleted is in fact removed, and that remnants of it no longer exist 'in the cloud'? Conversely, what guarantees are there that information that needs to be retained for given periods of time, or in perpetuity, will in fact be retained? Storage of information in the cloud is a feature that could be present in any or all of the political states described in the next section, and certainly introduces an additional component of complexity to the nature of organisational information architecture.

The development of cloud computing raises the possibility of the rationalisation of IT infrastructure of individual organisations, thereby introducing the possibility of shared services models. This fundamental feature provides an opening for so-called streamlining of service provision in the public sector, and in numerous jurisdictions around the world we are seeing shifts and changes in the make-up of government bodies. Recognising that working 'in the cloud' has become a necessity for most organisations, the InterPARES Trust Project, an international research endeavour with the goal to examine the trustworthiness of 'records in the cloud' (Duranti and Rogers, 2019), recommended that, in order to avoid major pitfalls, organisations should pay particular attention to the terms and conditions of the service level agreements which they sign with cloud service providers.

Recordkeeping systems and tools

The requirements of the systems and tools that are developed and applied to achieve recordkeeping objectives are necessarily unique to each setting, as they have to take into account the specific objectives of the organisational context. However, it is important to emphasise that, despite the emergence and promotion of standalone systems for digital recordkeeping (EDRMS), use of such systems is unlikely to achieve more than limited success. Recordkeeping needs to be embedded in all information systems, otherwise recordkeepers will continue to be in the position of placing additional demands on individuals. Adding what will be perceived as burdensome and unnecessary tasks to already heavy workloads is not likely to be viewed favourably, and achieving recordkeeping objectives will be partial at best. Recordkeepers cannot depend solely on the individuals who understand why recordkeeping is important and necessary, as the risks of non-compliance are too great.

Assessment techniques

The approach to analysis of this area that is set out in ISO15489, and based on the original DIRKS methodology, is termed 'appraisal'. ISO15489 explains appraisal as a combination of insight into the organisational context coupled with identification of requirements for records to be created and captured (ISO15489-1 7.1).

This will identify the gaps relating to recordkeeping requirements and should include a comprehensive understanding of organisational information systems. If this work has already been carried out, then it can be used to provide insight into corporate information governance. We suggest two alternative approaches here, which will be much less resource intensive to carry out. They should not be regarded as substitutes for the analysis required in ISO15489, as they will not identify requirements for records.

Profiling

Building a profile of your organisation's IT infrastructure will enable you to sketch the outlines of the overall information architecture and provide insight into existing attitudes toward information security, whether or not this has been explicitly documented. Profiling can be carried out without access to the inner workings of the IT department and reflects the perspective of users, rather than the specialist, insider views more commonly presented.

Davenport's (1997) model of political states provides imagery which is easy to work with and to communicate to others, because of the likelihood of there being a shared understanding of what the terminology means. The models do not explicitly acknowledge recordkeeping concerns, but that need not be a barrier to adapting them to suit our purposes. The following are the five political states:

1 Information Federalism: 'An approach ... based on consensus and negotiation on the organisation's key information elements and reporting structures' (Davenport et al., 1992, 56). This state provides the ideal records management environment, one in which an overall, inclusive approach (i.e. not driven solely by the IT department) has been taken to developing the information architecture. This will be reflected in the decisions made relating to access and security restrictions.

2 Information Feudalism: 'The management of information by individual
   business units or functions which define their own information needs
   and report only limited information to the overall corporation'
   (Davenport et al., 1992, 56). Organisations reflecting this political state
   can be thought of as collections of cottage industries, possibly operating
   in competition with each other, with synergies seeming to occur by
   accident rather than design. Co-operation and collaboration between
   these small entities will be piecemeal. From a records management
   perspective this would be a disaster. There would be isolated pockets of
   recordkeeping, but little certainty of being able to guarantee that records
   were being created and maintained to provide evidence of organisational
   accountability.
3 Information Monarchy: 'The definition of information categories and
   reporting structures by the firm's leaders, who may or may not share the
   information willingly after collecting it' (Davenport et al., 1992, 56). The
   infrastructure reflected in this model will be one in which emphasis is
   placed on the creation and maintenance of records, and their
   management within official systems, but subsequent access to those
   records will not be primarily governed by work-related needs. The end
   result may well be the development of parallel personal information
   systems, in addition to the organisation-wide systems, which of course
   pose new sets of security threats and risks.
4 Information Anarchy: 'The absence of any overall information
   management policy, leading individuals to obtain and manage their own
   information' (Davenport et al., 1992, 56). Sadly, many Australian and
   New Zealand organisations are likely to be described as operating in this
   anarchic state. If there is a recordkeeping policy it is unlikely to be taken
   seriously, promoted or supported by senior management. The working
   environment will be characterised by employees developing their own
   information systems in order to carry out their work. To use continuum
   language, most activity will be taking place in the first (create) and
   second (capture) dimensions, with no formal systems operating in the
   third (organise) dimension.
5 Technocratic Utopia: 'A heavily technical approach to information
   management stressing categorisation and modelling of an organisation's
   full information assets, with heavy reliance on emerging technologies'
   (Davenport et al., 1992, 56). We usually refer to this as *technological*
   utopia, to emphasise the 'emerging technologies' component of the
   model. Thinking about a technological utopia draws attention to those
   situations where so much energy and resources are invested in a magic

bullet that will solve all the organisation's records related problems. However, the magic bullet of EDRMS is being acknowledged to be increasingly problematic; the magic bullets of digital archives repositories are gathering dust ... The list will doubtless go on and on. This utopian vision is a very attractive one, but of course quite contrary to our vision in this book. It is also interesting to reflect on the first component of the original definition quoted above, which refers to information assets. *Categorisation and modelling of an organisation's full information assets* certainly has connotations of the very technocratic (perhaps autocratic) nature of our traditional approaches to records management. These are the very types of activities that our recordkeeping informatics approach seeks either to eliminate or at least to rebalance.

Although the models predate the cloud computing environment, this does not mean that they are no longer relevant. We just need to be aware that underpinning all of them is a further layer that needs to be identified, namely, the extent to which services are being outsourced and/or shared with other organisations, and the consequent risks to recordkeeping. Davenport's models of information states are still valid in today's more complex environment, although it is increasingly challenging to discern which model predominates. Real detective work will be needed to gather enough information to provide meaningful insight into the situation.

There are three main areas to consider when undertaking profiling:

1 Reflect on your own experiences as a user. To accomplish your work-related tasks, do you have to log in to multiple systems? For instance, working in a university, you may be using the same username and password, but have to enter that information whenever you want to access the student record system, the library, the online learning environment and so on. Does data entered in one system automatically update another business system? For example, in that university setting, if a student changes their address in their student record, is that reflected in their library record? Thinking about the answer to these questions will give you some insight into the overall coherence of your organisation's information architecture, and an understanding that what may appear to be seamless is in fact being cobbled together beneath a common interface.

2 A more fundamental question is whether you have access to the information you need to carry out your responsibilities, and asking that question of other employees. This is the key information that will

provide insight into the dimensions of power and control that are
particularly reflected in the information federalism, feudalism and
monarchy models.

3   A further question is whether you and/or other employees tend to
develop 'personal' systems to track and record information needed to
carry out work responsibilities. These systems can range from complex
databases to relatively simple spreadsheets, and proliferation of these
may well reflect the state of 'information anarchy' described above.

Policy analysis

Decisions reflecting corporate IT governance attitudes will be reflected in the
IT department's policies and procedures, whether they are documented or
not. The following are examples of policy decisions that will impact on the
way that people work, and may prompt unofficial workarounds:

- The use of firewalls and application of spam filters. Are settings
appropriate? Do they block inappropriate content or do they prevent
people carrying out work-related responsibilities? Are the steps taken to
minimise risks acceptable, or do they compromise the receipt of work-
related e-mails?
- Setting size limits, on e-mail inboxes for instance. How is this enforced?
Does it result in systematic deletion of e-mails so that work can proceed?
- Measures taken to protect information from unauthorised access. For
instance, in a case-work setting, restricting retrieval of information
relating to individuals by blocking access to name data fields. Do
employees develop their own workarounds which pose greater risks to
security, such as using the person's name in file titling?
- Permissions for employees to use their own devices (ranging from USB
keys to mobile smartphones) to connect with organisational systems and
for work-related purposes. The so-called BYOD (bring your own device)
movement has gained a lot of attention (The Littler Report, 2012
provides a useful overview of issues and responses) and is one area of
policy which is likely to be flagrantly disregarded if it does not fit with
social realities. Is your organisation's policy realistic, given the
proliferation of these devices?

Identifying areas where people, whether intentionally or unintentionally,
break official rules or circumvent corporate systems by introducing
unauthorised, local 'innovations' (or 'deviations', as they are often perceived

by those who made the rules and systems) is a very important step towards designing and implementing systems that *work*. As pointed out by sociologists and communication researchers, organisations continuously negotiate between two opposite impulses, one directed towards formalisation, normalisation and stability (i.e. centripetal impulse) and the other character-ised by resistance, idiosyncrasy and ad hoc innovation (i.e. centrifugal impulse) (Spinuzzi, 2003). When policies are decided without proper consultation of all involved parties, or when technologies that are not a 'good fit' with the culture of a workplace are nevertheless imposed, it is almost inevitable that users will develop 'their own rules' to cope with the rigidity of the system. As Bowker and Star (1999) wrote:

> Imposed standards will produce workarounds. Because imposed standards cannot account for every local contingency, users will tailor the standardized forms, information systems, schedules, and so forth to meet their needs.
>
> (Bowker and Star, 1999, 159)

Records professionals should not disregard or dismiss these workarounds as 'bad' practices. On the contrary, in their capacity as 'mediators' between centripetal and centrifugal forces (Foscarini, 2010) they should pay special attention to the new or adapted tools and practices emerging at the sites where the work gets done. According to soft systems methodology – whose way of reasoning is in line with that followed in this book (for more information see especially Chapter 9) – in order to improve a 'problem situation' all perspectives, official and unofficial, should be taken into account and used to find some 'accommodation' that everyone in the organisation will be able to understand and support.

Interventions

The development of profiles, together with analysis of IT policies and the ways they are implemented, should provide a way to determine:

- the characteristics of corporate information governance in your organisation
- the implications of corporate information governance for records management.

Alternatively, if the DIRKS methodology as described by ISO15489 has already been applied, this information may be used for insight into this level three factor; that is, instead of being used for profiling, it would be considered in conjunction with policy analysis. The next step is to effect change, which will involve working collaboratively with the IT department. How to go about doing this is primarily a question of relationship building. The first strategy we suggest is to learn to speak their language – i.e. get up to speed with the IT basics. This is much easier said than done, and necessitates really focusing on what's important. We are bombarded with information *about* IT, as consumers, as employees and as decision makers. If you have a good grasp of the key fundamentals then you are much better placed to be able to sift the wheat from the chaff, and to contribute to infrastructure decisions. From the corporate IT governance perspective, the most important area on which to zero in is cloud computing. This really is a game changer, and records managers need to be able to participate in discussion and decision making.

In order to participate, you have to be informed, so we recommend the NIST (National Institute of Standards and Technology) report (Mell and Grance, 2011). This report on cloud computing is just seven pages long and is essential reading. It first identifies the basic characteristics of cloud computing and then provides concise definitions of the three service models: Software as a Service, Platform as a Service and Infrastructure as a Service. Each of these service models has different implications for what the customer organisation controls, so understanding the model that is in place or proposed will indicate the dimensions of what is (to be) outsourced. The final section in the report identifies the different deployment models, namely private, community, public and hybrid (p. 3). The *private cloud* deployment model is infrastructure set up for use by a single organisation. A *community cloud* is infrastructure for a specific group of customers, perhaps government departments, with common requirements. The *public cloud* is a model that most of us will be familiar with: infrastructure that can be used by anyone – Google Docs, for instance. The *hybrid cloud* is defined as 'a composition of two or more distinct cloud infrastructures (private, community, or public) that remain unique entities, but are bound together by standardised or proprietary technology that enables data and application portability (e.g. cloud bursting for load balancing between clouds)' (Mell and Grance, 2011, 3).

It is clear that the risks which records professionals have to be able to discuss will vary according to the service model and deployment model proposed or in place. Being armed with a basic understanding of the main features of each will enable a much more informed conversation to take place. We have to be able to demonstrate that we do have a part to play in that conversation, and hopefully, in so doing, we will start to lay the foundations for respect for our specialist expertise.

Another key strategy is not to wait to be invited into the IT department, but to take the initiative and invite their participation in the recordkeeping function. Forming a committee or steering group for recordkeeping, consisting of key stakeholders in the organisation (as suggested in Chapter 2), is a very effective way of building mutual respect; including IT representatives in that group is essential. This is particularly important in organisational settings where a low value has been accorded to records and recordkeeping, as discussed in Chapter 2. In this case, developing networks and relationships throughout the organisation will be a very important strategy, and the formation of this type of group is an essential component.

Summary and conclusions

It is critical that records professionals are aware of decision making relating to corporate information governance, and alert to its implications. The features of the organisational IT environment will impact on the ways that people behave and interact with information, and therefore influence the creation and maintenance of records. It is essential that the implications for users are taken into account, and that the inevitability is recognised of workarounds or even sabotage if governance decisions do not support efficient and effective working. The tensions between risk mitigation (a centripetal impulse) and ease of working (which may require centrifugal means) are analogous to those that recordkeepers are familiar with, namely, balancing access requirements against the need to protect information in accordance with social and organisational imperatives. Being a part of the conversation with IT is essential to understanding the rationale behind decisions that are made.

The particular challenge associated with assessing this area relates to the quantity of technical detail which you are likely to face. We recommend approaching information architecture from the user perspective, rather than attempting to navigate the intricacies from an IT perspective. Policies too must be considered from the perspectives of users, in order to identify unintended consequences which would impact on recordkeeping practices.

Note

1   https://www.rimpa.com.au/rimpa-live-annual-convention/call-for-papers/

References

Allen, B. R. and Boynton, A. C. (1991) Information Architecture: in search of efficient flexibility, *MIS Quarterly*, **15** (4), 435–45.

Bowker, G. and Star, S. L. (1999) *Sorting Things Out: classification and its consequences*, MIT Press.

Davenport, T. H. (1997) *Information Ecology: mastering the information and knowledge environment*, Oxford University Press.

Davenport, T. H., Eccles, R. G. and Prusak, L. (1992) Information Politics, *Sloan Management Review*, Fall, 53–65.

DLM Forum (2012) What Does Successful Information Governance Across Europe Look Like? What role should the DLM Forum take? Draft Version 0.3, www.dlmforum.eu/index.php?option=com_jotloader&view=categories&cid=48_76ec42296279d56983d653206bf50a12&Itemid=150 [accessed 21 January 2013].

Duranti, L. and Rogers, D. (eds) (2019) *Trusting Records in the Cloud*, Facet Publishing.

EDRM (2011) *How the Information Governance Reference Model (IGRM) Complements ARMA International's Generally Accepted Recordkeeping Principles (GARP®)*, www.edrm.net/resources/edrm-white-paper-series/igrm-garp [accessed 21 January 2013].

Foscarini, F. (2010) Understanding the Context of Records Creation and Use: 'Hard' versus 'soft' approaches to records management, *Archival Science*, **10** (4), 389–407.

Information and Records Management Society (IRMS) (2012) *Conference 2012 Speaker Information*, www.irms.org.uk/previousconferences/conference2012/2012speakersessions [accessed 18 September 2013].

International Organization for Standardization (ISO) (2001) ISO15489-1:2015 Information and documentation – Records management. Part 1: General.

International Organization for Standardization (ISO) and International Electrotechnical Commission (2008) ISO/IEC 38500:2008 Corporate governance of information technology.

The Littler Report (2012) *The 'Bring Your Own Device' to Work Movement: engineering practical employment and labor law compliant solutions*, www.littler.com/files/press/pdf/TheLittlerReport-TheBringYourOwnDeviceToWorkMovement.pdf [accessed 20 January 2013].

Mell, P. and Grance, T. (2011) The NIST Definition of Cloud Computing, Special Publication 800-145, National Institute of Standards and Technology, http://csrc.nist.gov/publications/nistpubs/800-145/SP800-145.pdf [accessed 20 January 2013].

Oliver, G. (2008) Information Culture: exploration of differing values and attitudes to information in organizations, *Journal of Documentation*, **64** (3), 363–85.

RIMPA (2012) *Information Governance*, http://inforum.net.au/ [accessed 17 October 2012].

Spinuzzi, C. (2003) *Tracing Genres Through Organizations: a sociocultural approach to information design*, MIT Press.

Stuart, K. and Bromage, D. (2010) Current State of Play: records management and the cloud, *Records Management Journal*, **20** (2), 217–25.

Yeo, G. (2018) *Records, Information and Data: exploring the role of record-keeping in an information culture*, Facet Publishing.

PART 5

CHAPTER 8

The metalevels: language and trust

This chapter is concerned with two features that can be related to any of the three ICF levels, namely, language and trust. The first part of the chapter introduces the idea of language as a socially constructed phenomenon. After examining the impact of the English language on recordkeeping it considers the local usage of certain terms by the members of specific workplace communities (i.e. their 'vernacular') and the relationship among different professional/technical languages, or jargons, within organisations. One of the purposes of this section is to uncover the rhetorical and social aspects of writing and speaking in the workplace. The underlying framework is provided by ideas derived from Rhetorical Genre Studies (RGS). Readers who wish to know more about the genre approach will find a dedicated section in Chapter 9 (pp. 160–2).

The second part of the chapter explores the notion of trust in the context of the ICF, in particular, people's trust in recordkeeping systems and processes. In Chapter 3 we considered another aspect of trust as reflected in preferences for different types of information: the likelihood of people placing more trust in their social network as a source of information as opposed to textual resources, and vice versa. In this chapter the focus is on shared practices and perceptions of those practices. In particular we will examine whether employees trust the systems that have been established within their organisations to manage records. The section begins by discussing archival perspectives on trust and trustworthiness, and identifies initiatives that have been developed to demonstrate trust, particularly by the digital preservation community. As our information culture perspectives are concerned with the ways that people feel and behave, our focus then turns to discussion of the consequences of lack of trust in organisational systems. Assessment techniques acknowledge the existing tools and methods that have been developed to address this area, but encourage going further, to find out how users regard the systems that have been set up, and the section on interventions explains the notion of reflective practice.

Another objective of the sections on assessment and interventions, and of the chapter as a whole, is to show how records professionals can contribute to making language more suitable to their purposes.

Language as a social fact

This section explores the effects of using a particular language – in terms of linguistic stocks (e.g. one's native tongue) as well as professional or technical languages (e.g. archival terminology) – in relation to the creation, use and maintenance of recorded information in organisations. The underlying assumption is that language is an integral part of our world and, as such, is socially constructed by speakers and listeners through their ongoing interactions in specific settings. Thus, language is a living, dynamic phenomenon which permeates all aspects of life – and all levels of our ICF – in that communication, whether written, oral or sign based, is essential to enable collective activities. The notion of language as a social fact (or act, if we want to stress the idea that language does not exist outside of its instantiations) reflects a certain philosophical view (namely, a constructivist understanding of social life) that is not shared by all language theorists.

Langue versus parole

The French sociologist Pierre Bourdieu (1991) explained that language may be considered from two fundamentally different viewpoints. One involves looking at it as a self-sufficient system of signs, independently of any actual realisations of the system by particular speakers. This perspective – which the Swiss linguist Ferdinand de Saussure named *langue* – may usefully be applied to analyse linguistic expressions as abstract entities, in isolation from the specific social conditions in which they are used. The other way of dealing with language matters refers to observing how people speak and write, and how they listen and read, in actual, socio-historically situated circumstances. In this case, language becomes 'performance' (Noam Chomsky) or *parole* (Saussure) and its study may reveal social tensions and power issues that would otherwise remain unaccounted for. The latter is the approach taken by Bourdieu (1991), and is also the one we have adopted in this book, as our purpose is to investigate attitudes, practices and worldviews that shape and are in turn shaped by the language we use.

This brief foray into linguistic theory may be viewed as a metaphor of the current state of records management studies. Most of our literature focuses on the *langue* of records management, that is, ideal representations of what a 'good' recordkeeping system *should* look like, what control mechanisms *should* be in place, how records creators and records managers *should* perform their tasks, independently of the specific conditions in which they act. This book and the assessment techniques it suggests are an invitation to change our approach (from prescriptive, or normative, to descriptive, or exploratory) and turn our attention to the *parole*, the actual manifestations of recordkeeping practices, with all the different 'dialects' and 'accents' that real people bring into the 'official language' of the discipline.

English as a lingua franca

Since the middle of the 20th century, English has increasingly become a common means of communication, a *lingua franca*, for speakers of different first languages. Various political, economic, socio-cultural and technological factors are at the origin of this phenomenon, which is particularly visible in environments characterised by the presence of multiple languages and cultures, from international organisations to daily encounters involving people from different countries, in both our personal and professional lives. The internet is one of those spaces where the use of English as a *lingua franca* (ELF) is particularly extensive. Some researchers even believe that the structure of the English language would inherently be better suited to computer processing (see META, n.d.). In any event, the web is one of those places where most people resort to ELF as a convenient means of communication, without considering that in doing so they support the role of English as an 'invisible hegemonic force which exerts strong influence over the framing of the global world' (Evans, 2018).

Does English represent a threat to national languages? According to socio-linguists who make a distinction between 'languages for communication' and 'languages for identification', English is not – for the time being – replacing national languages as a cultural identifier and a carrier of interpersonal values (House, 2003). Nevertheless, as the dominant *lingua franca* the English language carries greater prestige and validity than other languages. Various research projects and consortia, including for instance META-NET (A Network of Excellence forging the Multilingual Europe Technology Alliance), have been established to develop language technologies that support and promote multilingualism (e.g. applications that enable automatic translation). The fear that, due to the widespread diffusion of ELF, less powerful linguistic groups might disappear – at least from some sectors of society (e.g. digital media) – does exist. Because language is a social phenomenon and translation is a complex exercise, where equivalence is always approximate, it is unlikely that technology alone will re-establish some balance within the linguistic marketplace.

In the recordkeeping domain – which is a highly culture-dependent domain, as this book has been trying to demonstrate – the pervasiveness of English terms and Anglicism is well known. For instance, the expression 'records management' does not have an exact equivalent in other languages; thus, it is widely used all over the world in lieu of local terms or expressions which would not convey precisely the same meaning (e.g. *Schriftgutverwaltung* in German, or *gestione dell'archivio corrente* in Italian). By adopting English terminology, non-English countries also end up adopting (and reinforcing) the culturally specific ideas underlying that terminology. In fact, the overall discipline of records management, independently of the region in which it is practised or taught, appears to have been heavily influenced by the Anglo-Saxon understanding of it. EDRMS, which have been conceived and are still primarily developed in Anglophone countries, are today deployed all over the world; and the international standard ISO15489 is based on the Australian standard AS 4390-1996. Each community of users has adapted the ideas and methods embedded in those intellectual and material tools. Translating ISO15489 into several languages has been quite challenging, and this need to translate may influence the future development of the standard. Countries that have invested resources in translation are not likely to encourage substantial revision of content, for instance. This is a factor that is raised repeatedly in international debate about updating the standard. Nevertheless, beyond the influence of country-specific legal frameworks and local traditions, managing records seems to be an activity profoundly affected by the Anglo-Saxon model.

In his study of cultures, sociologist Geert Hofstede (2001) categorised the organisational configuration typical of Anglo-Saxon countries as 'implicitly structured'. The 'market model' that is the instantiation of such a cultural type would normally be characterised by 'narrow power distance' and 'weak uncertainty avoidance'. As we saw in Chapter 3, the latter are the cultural dimensions that Hofstede considers crucial to determine the character of an organisation. Power distance has to do with centralisation versus decentralisation of authority and power. A narrow power distance is an indicator of flat, unstructured or partly structured internal hierarchies, great delegation of powers, communication that flows in all directions and easy access to people and information. Uncertainty avoidance involves the degree to which organisations rely on rules, technologies and other kinds of constraints to keep the fear of the unknown under control. When this parameter is weak the organisation has little formalisation of practices in written policies and procedures and is particularly amenable to change.

Language determines the way in which people see the world; and the way the world appears to them determines their language and influences any other cultural tools. Now, by adopting the expression 'records management' – which was developed in 'market model' countries – organisations characterised by different combinations of cultural dimension indicators might experience some friction. For example, in 'full bureaucracies' (which, according to Hofstede, would score high in both power distance and uncertainty avoidance), the introduction of that terminology and the kinds of responsibilities and practices it involves would imply a renegotiation of the profile of the individuals entrusted with the management of current records. At the same time, it would also contribute to loosening some forms of control that traditionally characterise such bureaucracies (e.g. a central registry system), or to emphasising a divide between the records management and archival professions which may not exist in the countries that Hofstede associates with the full bureaucratic type (i.e. Japan, Latin-Mediterranean and Islamic countries).

We have already mentioned the limitations of Hofstede's ideas and the dangers involved in his generalisations (see pp. 10 and 68). However, even without drawing on his matrix, it is still important to keep in mind that when the same terms are used by people belonging to different countries, organisational models or archival traditions, one cannot assume that those terms will share the exact same meaning that they have in the countries and traditions where they had been coined. With translation, the situation is even more complex, as the 'source culture' and the 'target culture' (as translators call the context of the word or text to be translated and that into which the word or text is meant to be translated, respectively) may have little in common (Baker, 2001). It is therefore important to always define your terms, even the most habitual ones such as 'record' or 'file', especially when dealing with multinational teams or participating in international events.

'Vernacular' and discourse practices

As the American anthropologist Clifford Geertz (1983) suggested, 'the vocabularies in which [individuals within an organisation] converse offer a way of gaining access to the sorts of mentalities at work in [it]' (p. 157). Both for the researcher who tries to gain insight into the worldview of an organisation and for the practitioner who is interested in understanding how things work in his or her workplace, paying attention to the 'vernacular of shared terms' (Smart, 2006, 153) employed by community members in talking about their activities is important. Novices, especially, will need to learn those shared terms and how they are used in the organisation they have joined, as a way of becoming full participants in it. Experienced practitioners may have more difficulty recognising their workplace's vernacular, as they will tend to use it routinely and unreflectively. However, if they wish to contribute to improving their organisation's *discourse practices* (i.e. work practices, together with the written, oral and other symbol-based tools used by professional communities to accomplish their work, including the management of corporate records), both newcomers and old-timers should become aware of the 'key terms that seem, when their meaning is unpacked, to light up a whole way of going at the world' (Geertz, 1983, 157).

In his study of the discourse practices in place at the Bank of Canada and their evolution over almost two decades, Graham Smart (2006) offers several examples of the bank's vernacular. For instance, the bank employees whom he interviewed would recurrently and unknowingly refer to the 'Old Bank' versus the 'New Bank' (153–4). When using those expressions, insiders knew what they meant, as everyone in the organisation shared the feeling that there was a moment when the bank became more transparent and open to the outside world (that moment coincided with the adoption of a new communication strategy).

The linguistic analysis carried out by Fiorella in her study of central banks (Foscarini, 2009) revealed that in one of the organisations studied 'records classification' was systematically replaced with 'folder structure' when the bank's employees would talk about electronic records. Although both classification tools (the one applied to paper-based records and the new one developed for the electronic environment) had the same function and were based on almost the same principles, it was clear that the new technology, and the relevant IT terminology, had had an impact on the way people thought and talked about classification. In another case study site, classification was interpreted as one of the descriptive elements of the bank's finding aid (thus related to the bank's historical holdings, rather than its current records). Even after Fiorella had explained what she meant by records classification, employees would still discuss how they managed the bank's historical archives. This misunderstanding teaches us two lessons: first, the meaning of our professional vocabulary should never be taken for granted, as each workplace will develop its own understanding of recordkeeping terms (see the next section); second, the vernacular usage of a term will always tend to prevail over other, even more widely recognised, usages.

The archival jargon

Because the records management and archival discipline (for those of us who see it as a single body of knowledge) involves several, quite distinct traditions, and over the course of time has been associated to a number of other disciplinary perspectives from which it has drawn various features (e.g. diplomatics, law, history, librarianship and, more recently, information science and IT), the professional or technical terminology that we here call 'archival jargon' (where 'archival' is used as an overarching term that includes all recordkeeping functions, and 'jargon' is not meant to have negative connotations) is quite a contested realm. As mentioned earlier in this chapter, even basic terms like 'record', 'document', 'file', 'classification' cannot be employed without at the same time specifying what we mean by them, as the circumstances of use, which are ever changing, will influence the relationship between the writer/speaker and the reader/listener.

It is common experience to run into misunderstandings when, for instance, IT specialists, experts from any department or business area and records professionals meet to discuss recordkeeping requirements in a digital environment. Professional education, previous positive or negative experiences with managing electronic records or systems, country of origin and any other existing cultural factors will influence each participant's interpretation of the issues at stake. For the IT specialist, 'record' may mean any entry into a database, or 'an ordered set of fields, usually stored contiguously' (according to the definition provided by a computer dictionary, FOLDOC, 2002); the area experts may think that only their final, official documents are 'records'; while the records specialist may make reference to any of the 14 different definitions of a record included in the InterPARES 2 Terminology Database (n.d.) or to a 'local' definition developed within the organisation.

Should we blame our archival jargon for being imprecise? As this chapter has tried to show by drawing on linguistics and genre studies, even the most technical languages come from a complex history of negotiations of meanings and are subject to continuous renegotiations. All we can do to avoid misrepresentations of what we say is to describe our specific usages of certain terms in our policies, manuals of procedure and guidelines explaining how to use our tools, as well as in any discussions which we may have with audiences who may not share our professional background. In order to communicate effectively with such audiences it is also advisable to develop some familiarity with the jargons of other disciplines, particularly IT, as already emphasised in Chapter 7.

Writing and speaking in the workplace

An aspect of communication that tends to be overlooked when records issues are discussed is the rhetoric that is inherent in workplace writing and speaking. When we write a memo or a project proposal, when we draft and discuss in meetings a progress report and so on, we most of the time try to use persuasive arguments, so that our ideas will get support or the outcomes of the discussion will be favourable to us. Records manifest such a rhetorical dimension through their content, structure, time and place of creation, addressee(s), authorship and other features that disciplines such as diplomatics and genre theory study, each in its own terms (Foscarini, 2012).

Exploring these issues in depth is outside the scope of this book. Our brief reference to rhetoric – or the social context in which communication takes place for the purpose of influencing that context – is just meant to reiterate that information is power (as stressed in Chapter 3 in relation to information sharing) and that our ability to exercise power through records rests with our rhetorical and genre knowledge, that is, our individual understanding of what specific types of records do and how they do it (Bazerman and Prior, 2004).

Writing in the workplace is mostly a collaborative activity. It is indeed rare to find 'solo authors' of corporate records. A report written by city employees on construction activities may include contributions by engineers, city planners, administrators, lawyers and so on. As research on professional writing suggests (Beaufort, 2008), this intertwining of different areas of expertise, different writing styles and different objectives has an impact on people's sense of ownership towards their texts. While it is essential to recognise that our records are not 'ours' but, rather, belong to the organisation for which we work (as discussed in Chapters 1 and 2), there may be psychological consequences related to collaborative writing that should not be under-estimated. Experiencing loss of control over your texts, not knowing who your readers are going to be, not being able to see the final version of the record you contributed to: all these situations might alter the rhetorical power we mentioned above, thus engendering disengagement, limited or no emotional involvement with your writing activities. Such attitudes might in turn impact on the effectiveness, accuracy and reliability of your records and, as we know well, these are very relevant aspects of recordkeeping.

Trust and trustworthiness

The nature of trust and trustworthiness has been the subject of much research and debate both in the records and archival disciplines and the broader information environment. The intensity of discussion has increased in conjunction with the proliferation of digital technologies. One high-profile project addressing this area is the research into the long-term preservation of authentic electronic records led by Luciana Duranti at the University of British Columbia, InterPARES.

To date four iterations of this project have been completed, involving teams of researchers (both academics and practitioners) from around the globe. Outputs include the development of theory as well as strategies and policies for organisations of all types. The conceptual framework of InterPARES involves primarily archival science and diplomatics, the latter being a scientific approach to the study of the form and function of documents in order to establish their authenticity. Accordingly, the definition of trustworthiness proposed by the project ('The accuracy, reliability and authenticity of a record' [InterPARES 2 Terminology Database, n.d.]) focuses on observable and measurable characteristics of the records as objects.

The digital preservation community has also recognised the importance of being able to provide assurance that repositories developed for the long-term storage of digital information can be relied on, and the need to build a relationship of trust with stakeholders. This recognition has resulted in the development of a clear strategy to demonstrate trustworthiness, namely, audit and certification programmes. The first of these programmes was initiated in 2000 by the Research Libraries Group (RLG) and resulted in the development of a framework of attributes and responsibilities for Trusted Digital Repositories (RLG, 2002). Shortly after this a German network of excellence in digital preservation was established; their work included the identification of criteria for trustworthy digital archives (Nestor, 2008). DRAMBORA (Digital Repository Audit Method Based On Risk Assessment), developed as an outcome of pilot audits of digital repositories, is a self-assessment methodology approaching digital preservation from a risk management perspective (DCC, 2008).

Despite these large-scale, international projects, issues of trust are still unresolved. Perhaps this is because there has been more of an emphasis on the systems and technology involved, and the complexity of the people issues has not yet been fully appreciated. A step in the right direction is Jenny Bunn et al.'s (2016) study for InterPARES Trust (i.e. the fourth iteration of the project) of 'User Perceptions of Born-Digital Authenticity', the main findings of which are now included in Duranti and Rogers (2019).

To understand what it means to focus on perceptions rather than technical specifications, consider the case of digital repositories. Archival institutions worldwide have invested considerable amounts of resources into the development of digital archives. However, it appears that at least in the government sector the agencies that are traditional depositors have not rushed to transfer their records (see Cunningham, 2011 for a frank assessment of the situation at the National Archives of Australia). In interviews with records managers in New Zealand it was suggested to Gillian that one reason for this hesitation could be lack of trust. In particular, the IT people working in government departments who are key decision makers in the transfer of electronic records may not trust the capability and competency of archivists. Accordingly, a survey was conducted to try to find out the perceptions of IT professionals with respect to archivists. The findings of this survey showed differences in the perception of trustworthiness in terms of abilities to manage paper versus digital records: IT professionals were more likely to trust archivists to know what to do with paper than to know what to do with digital information (Oliver et al., 2011).

Audit

How can we trust that records created and managed in the digital environment have the characteristics mandated by ISO15489, that they have integrity, are authentic, are usable and can be relied on? The standard's approach to addressing this question centres on monitoring and auditing, recommending that this be undertaken regularly (ISO15489-1, 10). This clause has its origins in DIRKS, in this case Step H Post Implementation Review (DIRKS, 2007), although it is noteworthy that the standard refers to an additional feature that needs to be examined: user satisfaction. Considering what user satisfaction means provides more insight into the nuances of trust, or lack of trust, that are unlikely to be identified in an audit process but that can be addressed if we are perceptive enough.

Mistrust

The complexity of trust (see MacNeil, 2000; Cook et al., 2009), the international community's continued attempts to address the issue and the resourcing required to adequately monitor and audit should not be taken to mean that we can contribute nothing in day-to-day recordkeeping. On the contrary, this is a crucially significant area that we can do something about *on a daily basis*, and yet more often than not we fail to do so. The reasons for this are grounded firmly in the disjuncture that arises when we fail to address the 'people problem' and focus instead on the implementation of 'best practice'. To put it simply, the area where individual records professionals can achieve a great deal is in building positive relationships with users. More specifically, we need to establish a relationship of trust so that employees will be confident that the systems developed and implemented to manage records can be relied on and will serve their work-related purposes. A shift in trust can affect all levels of the ICF, both in a positive and in a negative sense.

Working in collaboration with other information professionals is a clearly stated aim of recordkeeping informatics; this will be possible only if there is mutual trust and respect on all sides. We often focus on the inequities of recordkeeping vis-à-vis other organisational functions and departments, but do not seem to translate that into positive actions that can start to address the situation. The section on interventions urges a critically reflective approach to professional practice, which we believe is essential to achieve change.

If users do not trust organisational recordkeeping systems, or if they lack confidence in them, the outcome will be quite simple – systems will not be used. The consequences of that would be disastrous for recordkeeping. It does not matter how well systems have been designed, how much has been invested in them or what the legislative drivers are: if they are not trusted, organisational records will remain with individuals or workgroups.

A case in point

A classic example of this situation was witnessed at a large university. While interviewing users throughout the organisation, Gillian was shown a series of hard-copy files in one work unit. The interviewees recounted with great glee that these files were 'their own' and contained legally important documents, namely signed contracts for very high dollar-value service agreements, together with all related correspondence. Furthermore, the records manager was kept in the dark about these, as the workgroup made certain to send an insignificant component relating to these files for 'official filing', in order not to arouse any suspicions.

The deception was thus very deliberate in intent, and quite elaborate in execution. The explanation for this feral system, which was carefully hidden from view, was that the workgroup did not trust the records management staff. The members of the workgroup had a high level of regard for the need to create and maintain records, but a very low level of regard for those designated as organisational recordkeepers.

The reason for all this was reported as being a single past incident that had occurred at least a couple of years before. Until that point staff had been meticulous about sending all contracts and related correspondence to the records management department. They understood that the records would be retained for the statutory period (the organisation had developed a retention and disposal schedule), and had been assured that they would be consulted before destruction was carried out. However, when information was needed and the retrieval of a specific file was requested, no records had been forthcoming. The workgroup were at first informed that the records had been transferred to another storage location and there would be a delay in retrieval. Eventually, after repeated requests, they were informed that the records had been destroyed, but no supporting documentation was provided to substantiate this. From that point on, the workgroup effectively ceased to trust the recordkeeping function. When this account was repeated to the records manager, the incident was dismissed as 'nonsense' and the reaction was one of amusement more than anything else. No intention was expressed to follow up and investigate; the incident was simply laughed off with a comment that it was just typical behaviour from the people working in that unit.

We must be alert to the tales and anecdotes circulating about our services, and take steps to address them. It is often not even relevant whether an incident actually happened or not: the important thing is that people *believe* something happened, to the extent that it has a profound and ongoing effect on their work practices and cooperation with recordkeeping systems. Furthermore, in any large and complex organisation the negative impact from a single slip-up, real or imagined, will not be restricted to a single work unit. On the contrary, people talk to each other, and stories circulate, regardless of how true they are. Myths and legends are very persistent and are an acknowledged manifestation of an organisation's corporate culture (Hofstede, 2001, 382).

Moreover, attitudes and opinions will not be confined to particular features of recordkeeping, but will carry over to other systems and processes. In this instance, original signed contracts in hard-copy files were the bone of contention. But at the same time an organisation-wide EDRMS was being rolled out and it was clear from comments made by the interviewees that there was considerable scepticism about its chances of success. As we saw in Chapter 2, how users judge and talk about a system – their 'appropriation moves' (DeSanctis and Poole, 1994) – is very important to understanding how the system is actually being (or not being) used.

How should the records manager have reacted? Admittedly, it is a difficult situation, but defensiveness, however it is manifested, is neither appropriate nor helpful. The most important thing to do is to accept that a problem exists, and not necessarily to focus on the cause, which could have been a misunderstanding or a mistake on either side. For something that occurred a significant length of time ago, it is probably not a productive use of time to try to find out what actually happened. Instead, there should be a commitment to check (in ISO15489 language, to monitor and audit) the processes concerned, to take corrective action to ensure these are robust and to communicate this to the parties involved. There should be a commitment to work *with* the users (as opposed to doing things *to* them) and to listen to their concerns on an ongoing basis, with the clear aim of *building a relationship of trust* – in short, to act ethically and responsibly.

Ethical practice

In Chapter 7 we alluded to the importance of a clear ethical stance with which to inform decision making and to provide the right foundation for professional practice. It has been pointed out that there is not a clearly defined trust relationship between archivists and the public, partly due to lack of knowledge about what archivists actually do and why they do it (Dingwall, 2004). Understanding ethical principles and being able to put these into practice are critical concerns for records professionals and are key factors in establishing relationships of trust with users.

Given that records professionals (both records managers and archivists) are concerned with organisational and societal memory, it is not surprising that ethical issues are frequently debated in the professional literature (see, e.g. the writings of Richard Cox, 2006, 2011). Inevitably, discussion usually focuses on the high-profile cases and dilemmas which grab the headlines around the world (Arthur Anderson, Enron and WikiLeaks are just three examples). When records managers think about ethics, perhaps the predominant concern is whether they would act as whistle blowers, defined by Richard Cox as 'individuals who place the welfare of society and its inhabitants over their own' (2008, 1132), and attention therefore focuses on what sets of circumstances would prompt such controversial and courageous responses. Given the dramatic and stirring quality of this debate, it is perhaps easy to lose sight of the much more mundane daily activities and responsibilities that require ethical concerns to be taken into account and routinely applied.

Professional associations have addressed the need to promote ethical practice by developing codes of conduct which should identify the main behaviours that are expected of records professionals (Archives and Records Association, 2012, for instance), or by issuing statements explaining the nature of ethical practice (RIMPA, 2010). This Australian statement identifies the main features of ethical practice as being:

- Protecting accountability and the public interest
- Preserving records of continuing value
- Maintaining integrity
- Protecting rights and privileged information
- Supporting equitable and appropriate access to information
- Being objective and independent
- Acting competently
- Continuing to develop your knowledge, skills and competencies
- Satisfying your responsibilities to your employer / client
- Promoting recordkeeping and information management.

(RIMPA, 2010, 1)

These features are accompanied by clear and succinct explanations which are very much grounded in organisational realities and are thus well worth keeping at the forefront of one's mind. They are very relevant to daily practice, and ensuring that they are observed will greatly assist, over time, in building and maintaining a relationship of trust with users. Considering the details of the case described above, and assessing the actions and responses in the context of these ethical practice features, it is evident that the records manager could not be said to have been acting ethically.

In the last few years, the ethical dimension of recordkeeping has been enriched, thanks to discussions around diversity, inclusivity and a desire to reject the traditional models and principles which for centuries have perpetuated the views of those in positions of power, while suppressing the voice of the *other*. These discussions have been spurred by community-led archival initiatives and scholars' reflections on how to 'decolonise' the archives – that is, how to find ways to conceptualise and practise recordkeeping from perspectives that would be radically different to dominant ones, such as feminist, LGBTQ and disabled people's perspectives (see Ramirez, 2010; Flinn, 2011; Caswell and Cifor, 2016; Cifor and Wood, 2017; Brilmyer, 2018; Lee, 2019). The ICF embraces diversity and inclusivity by not promoting one particular approach to recordkeeping over others, and by recognising that multiple cultures of recordkeeping are not only possible but desirable. It will not have escaped the reader that the hegemony of the English language in all aspects of life, including recordkeeping – discussed in the first part of this chapter – speaks to forms of cultural imperialism and neo-colonialism of which records professionals need to be aware.

Assessment techniques

Assessing language

Capturing and analysing how people speak and write is a complex endeavour which requires knowledge of linguistic theories and methods. However, for the purpose of investigating information cultures, becoming aware of special usages of words and starting to understand the motives behind those usages is an important first step.

As a general suggestion, when you apply the techniques described earlier in relation to other components of the ICF, pay attention to the ways in which writers and speakers use English terms (if you are in a country whose mother tongue is not English, or if you work for an international or a multinational organisation where ELF is the working language) in formal and informal, written and oral communications (e.g. letters, e-mails, interview transcripts, presentations). Similarly, you note down words and expressions that have a special meaning in your workplace (the workplace vernacular).

One of the purposes of this exercise is to make communication more transparent in terms of what people want to achieve by writing or speaking in a given way (even when they are not aware of their rhetorical goals). Asking a direct question about (e.g. How do you make a persuasive argument? Do you know of any words or expressions that are recurrently used in this unit/organisation to mean something that only the people in this unit/organisation can understand?) may not yield the desired response. Sometimes a workplace vernacular becomes apparent when talking about work with friends or with people from other organisations, or with people who have a professional background that is different from your own. If a term that is obvious to you needs to be explained so as to make sense to others, that is a good sign that you are using the vernacular. It would also be recommendable to share the documents you intend to analyse (or your findings, in case you have a good grasp of this matter) with someone external to your organisation.

Assessing people's engagement or involvement with their activities (as discussed in relation to the effects of collaborative writing) is not less difficult than exploring other 'soft' aspects of their work. If a survey is used to assess behaviour, an effective way of asking questions about engagement is through 'scenarios', where respondents are invited to consider possible situations and choose the one that is closest to their reality. A scenario-based question exploring issues of engagement with information might sound like the following:

Please pick the statement that best describes your work situation:

1   At my workplace, I want to get my work done as soon as possible and don't want to spend extra time with information management tasks; but when I am at home, I don't mind spending time managing my personal information (e.g. Facebook, personal archiving).
2   I invest more time and energy in organising business information at my workplace than I do in my personal life when I am at home.
3   I tend to invest the same amount of time and effort in managing my personal information at home as I do with the management of business information at work.

Assessing trust

In order to really probe trust in recordkeeping systems it will be essential to communicate directly with users, rather than to concentrate solely on the systems and technologies involved. DIRKS and/or other analytical tools discussed in Chapter 1 provide the conventional approach to assessing the trustworthiness of recordkeeping systems and processes, so this is one avenue of approach. If DIRKS analysis or similar audit or review has already been carried out, the information gathered will be very useful. It may provide insight into problem areas that need to be addressed, and the activity itself can be used as a promotional tool to demonstrate trustworthiness.

However, even though an audit-type process may meet the requirements of an external regulatory body, it cannot be assumed that a successful outcome will necessarily demonstrate trust on the part of system users. Further investigation is essential, focused on exploring users' perceptions (whether correct or incorrect) of recordkeeping systems. The aim of the assessment techniques discussed here is to find out what people think about the trustworthiness of recordkeeping systems and processes, and not to assess the systems themselves.

Assessment of this metalevel characteristic can be incorporated into existing plans to conduct a survey or to interview users, but we also suggest a new technique: ethnography.

Survey

See Chapter 2 for general guidance about developing an online survey. A single, simple question may be enough to gain a perspective on the extent to which people trust recordkeeping systems:

- I am confident that I will be able to retrieve information that I have added to the organisational filing system in five years' time: Agree/Disagree.

The question should be tailored to the organisational context, for instance by substituting 'EDRMS' for 'organisational filing system', or more than one question should be developed if there are parallel paper and electronic systems. Responses to this question will flag whether or not trust in organisational systems is a problem area, but they will not explain why. Finding out why will involve talking to a diversity of people and listening to their concerns.

Interviews

See Chapter 2 for general comments about the use of interviews, both one on one and focus groups. Questions to probe people's views of the trustworthiness of recordkeeping systems can be developed according to the following pattern:

- Are you confident that you will be able to retrieve information from the organisational filing system in five years' time? If not, why not?

Again, questions should be tailored to the systems that are operational in the organisational environment. The time period of five years is specifically suggested because it should be far enough in the future for people to visualise the type of difficulties that may eventuate, without being too remote in the distant future.

Ethnography

Ethnography describes a particular research methodology, originating in anthropology, aimed at exploring cultural phenomena from within. Depending on the topic under investigation, ethnographic fieldwork may involve living in a remote area of the world alongside a particular ethnic minority, or can take place in an organisational setting. Investigation at organisational level would involve the researcher becoming a part of the organisation, for instance by actually working there, in order to be able to study and observe from within.

Records professionals can adopt a similar stance of ethnographic enquiry, which may prove very worthwhile not only in identifying the ICF characteristics of trust, but also in building strong relationships with users. Listen for the anecdotes, myths and legends that are circulating in your organisation. What are the consequences, if any, for recordkeeping? You will hear these stories only if you are truly embedded in the organisation, and not maintaining a separatist, back-room profile.

Depending on the size and complexity of your organisation, and resourcing constraints, it may be possible to actually work alongside your users so as to gain insight into particular information-intensive activities. For instance, in the university sector student administration services could be a suitable option. Stepping outside the boundaries of the records management function to experience working with recordkeeping systems from the other side will be enlightening and invaluable. Perhaps it would also be possible to develop a reciprocal programme, to involve users in working in the records department. This would contribute greatly to developing mutual trust and respect. It would also foster an effective kind of organisational learning which, differently from the learning associated with formal training measures, happens mostly tacitly and continuously through participating in shared practices. We discussed direct and indirect training issues in Chapter 6.

When work placement rotations are not a viable option, a much less drastic approach that can be taken is active participation in the social life of the organisation. Social occasions such as morning teas are good opportunities to become exposed to the tales and rumours that are circulating, and are important vehicles of enculturation. It is important to make a conscious effort to take part in the social life of the organisation, as by doing this you will increase your chances of hearing about concerns and thus be well placed to address them.

Interventions

As emphasised above in the discussion of language considerations, it is very important for records professionals to define their terms and reflect on where they come from, especially those 'boundary terms' that are used by more than one discipline. Archival dictionaries and glossaries can be consulted for the purpose of identifying the correct meaning(s) of records-related terms. Some are available online[1] and are extremely useful resources. However, no glossary or terminology database will ever tell you how a term is used *in your workplace*. Records managers are in an excellent position, together with their colleagues from other information-related areas (e.g. archivists, librarians and IT experts), to develop dictionaries or glossaries of records terminology for internal use. Such tools, which would provide anyone in the organisation with the local, situated meanings of commonly employed terms, should be 'living documents' and should be updated regularly.

Being able to respond to concerns relating to the second metalevel characteristic, people's trust in recordkeeping systems, will necessitate *reflective practice*. A detailed review of the theory of reflection is provided by M. Sarah Wickham (2010), who argues strongly for the need for archivists and records managers to develop such a type of practice. The concept of reflective practice originated with Professor Donald Schön (1983). Writing in the early 1980s, Schön was responding to a crisis in the public's confidence in professional knowledge, the end of unconditional acceptance that the professional always knows best. He argued that the complexity and uncertainty that now characterise society necessitate different patterns of behaviour; professionals have to be prepared to tailor their responses to fit different circumstances. Of particular relevance to records managers is his acknowledgement of 'strong' and 'weak' professionals (p. 298). The former are members of the old-established professions, such as physicians and architects. The latter (in which we can include records professionals) are those whose specialist knowledge does not have widespread recognition or understanding.

Schön summarised the differences in attitudes and behaviours between the old-style 'expert' and the new, reflective practitioner, which we have adapted slightly to be relevant to records professionals (Table 8.1).

Table 8.1 *Differences between old and new professional types (adapted from Schön, 1983, 300)*

Expert	Reflective practitioner
I am (or want to be) presumed to know best, and I must always retain that appearance, regardless of whether or not it is in fact true	I am presumed to be knowledgeable, but not exclusively so. What I don't know can be a source of new learning for all parties
I maintain a safe distance from users, and make sure I retain my role as the expert	I try to find out what users are thinking. I aim to earn their respect for my knowledge, in the course of working together
I expect deference from users in response to my professional persona	I seek real connections with users, and enjoy interacting with them, as a consequence of not having to maintain a professional persona

Lifelong learning

These ideas about the need for reflective practice have been further developed and applied to education. The underlying principle is that by reflecting on and analysing experiences the practitioner continues learning (lifelong learning). This theory has been enormously influential in educational settings, particularly where the aims of the programme are vocational, to develop professional practice. You may have experienced study assignments which have involved keeping a journal or blog, or required critical reflection on the literature of a given topic. Such assignments are designed to help develop students' ability to engage in reflective practice, but whether or not these skills are retained and honed after formal education finishes will probably vary according to the individual or other practice requirements. Professional associations provide continuing education or professional development opportunities which in general aim to promote lifelong learning. If the association offers licensing or credentialing of its members, often some sort of reflective journalling component is required as evidence that the practitioner is learning by analysing and reflecting on their experiences in the workplace.

Reflective practice and information culture

We see reflective practice as a crucial component for professional recordkeepers. Indeed, it is an essential for engagement with the information culture perspective, and nowhere is the need for this more striking than in consideration of this metalevel ICF factor. After first determining the situation with regard to users' trust of records systems, the next step is crucial. This involves seeking connections to users, learning from their experiences of recordkeeping systems and responding appropriately. This is quite different from rejecting users' views as not valid, or simply insisting that the way things are being done is the one and only correct way. That stance corresponds to the 'expert' in Table 8.1. Genuinely reflective practice involves attempting to understand activities from other perspectives, being open minded and ready to continue learning. These qualities will enable you to escape rigid, practitioner straightjackets which position recordkeepers in oppositional roles to their users. Reflective practice will help in developing systems to which users respond positively, rather than avoiding or sabotaging them.

Reflective practice should be underpinned by knowledge and understanding of ethical principles, as discussed above, so it is important to be aware of specific codes that are developed by your professional body. Cast your net widely, though, and look for comparable ethical codes or statements that may be relevant; in order to be able to really apply ethical practice, it is necessary to be confident that you clearly understand the principles involved.

Summary and conclusions

This chapter has provided an overview of two important factors that condition (but do not determine) records-making and recordkeeping in organisations: the language in which we speak and write as members of workplace communities, and trust in recordkeeping. Being deeply rooted in a socio-cultural layer that may extend beyond the boundaries of an individual organisation or a country, these metalevel factors may be hard to change, and any modifications may become recognisable only after long periods of time. One of the goals has been to raise awareness of the role played by language in society, and of its cultural, political, economic and symbolic underpinnings. From a critical understanding of the words we speak and of the technology available to communicate them, better uses of both may emerge.

The principle that recordkeeping systems must be trustworthy, and thus capable of ensuring the key characteristics of records as authentic, reliable, having integrity and being usable is widely acknowledged. Strategies to ensure trustworthiness have centred on monitoring and audit processes, often involving external regulatory bodies. However, there is potential for a significant gap between the certification of compliance and the perceptions of individual users with regard to the trustworthiness of systems. We need to make sure not only that our systems are trustworthy, but also that our users too share this trust. It is only in this way that activities will progress beyond the first two dimensions (create and capture) of the records continuum model.

Taking an information culture approach means that attention can be shifted to the gap between meeting audit requirements and users' perceptions, so highlighting any issues that impact on people's use of recordkeeping systems. It is a question not of how trustworthy recordkeeping systems are but, rather, of what users think about them. Thus, assessment techniques concentrate on finding out what users think of systems, and whether they are confident of being able to retrieve information in the future. In this chapter we also urged the social integration of the recordkeeper in the organisation, in order to be in tune with opinions, so that appropriate actions can be taken.

Remembering that this characteristic is a question of opinions and beliefs should help records professionals to respond positively and take appropriate actions. Being defensive and attempting to argue the rights and wrongs of a specific incident will not necessarily help in building positive relationships of trust. Awareness and understanding of ethical principles is essential, as is the development of reflective practice. As stated at the outset, this characteristic is very susceptible to change. That does not mean that change will be easy, but it does mean that the potential for change is in our hands, and this is an area where we can actively work to influence outcomes.

Note

1   See, for example, the Society of American Archivists' Glossary of Archival and
    Records Terminology at www2.archivists.org/glossary and the InterPARES
    Project's Terminology Database at
    www.interpares.org/ip2/ip2_terminology_db.cfm.

References

Archives and Records Association (2012) *ARA Code of conduct*,
    www.archives.org.uk/images/documents/ARACouncil/ARA_Code_of_Conduct_
    final.pdf [accessed 22 January 2013].

Baker, M. (ed.) (2001) *Routledge Encyclopedia of Translation Studies*, Routledge.

Bazerman, C. and Prior, P. (2004) *What Writing Does and How It Does It: an
    introduction to analyzing texts and textual practices*, Laurence Erlbaum Associates
    Publishers.

Beaufort, A. (2008) Writing in the Professions. In Bazerman, C. (ed.), *Handbook of
    Research on Writing: history, society, school, individual, text*, Lawrence Erlbaum
    Associates, 221–35.

Bourdieu, P. (1991) *Language and Symbolic Power*, Polity Press.

Brilmyer, G. (2018) Archival Assemblages: applying disability studies'
    political/relational model to archival description, *Archival Science*, **18** (2), 95-118.

Bunn, J., Brimble, S., Obelensky, S. and Wood, N. (2016) *Perceptions of Born Digital
    Authenticity*, EU28, Final Report. InterPARES Trust.
    https://interparestrust.org/assets/public/dissemination/EU28_20160718_
    UserPerceptionsOfAuthenticity_FinalReport.pdf [accessed 17 March 2020].

Caswell, M. and Cifor, M. (2016) From Human Rights to Feminist Ethics: radical
    empathy in archives, *Archivaria*, **81**, 23–43.

Cifor, M. and Wood, S. (2017) Critical Feminism in the Archives, *Journal of Critical
    Library and Information Studies*, **1** (2), https://doi.org/10.24242/jclis.v1i2.27.

Cook, K. S., Levi, M. and Hardin, R. (2009) *Whom Can We Trust? How groups,
    networks, and institutions make trust possible*, Russell Sage Foundation.

Cox, R. J. (2006) *Ethics, Accountability and Recordkeeping in a Dangerous World*, Facet
    Publishing.

Cox, R. J. (2008) Archival Ethics: the truth of the matter, *Journal of the American
    Society for Information Science and Technology*, **59** (7), 1128–33.

Cox, R. J. (2011) *Archival Anxiety and the Vocational Calling*, Litwin.

Cunningham, A. (2011) Good Digital Records Don't Just 'Happen': embedding
    digital recordkeeping as a component of business processes and systems,
    Archivaria, **71**, 21–34.

DeSanctis, G. and Poole, M. S. (1994) Capturing the Complexity in Advanced Technology Use: adaptive structuration theory, *Organization Science*, **5** (2), 121–47.

DCC (2008) *About Drambora*, www.repositoryaudit.eu/about/ [accessed 23 January 2013].

Dingwall, G. (2004) The Role of Archival Ethics Codes in Establishing Public Faith, *The American Archivist*, **67** (1), 11–30.

DIRKS Manual (2007) https://www.records.nsw.gov.au/recordkeeping/strategies-documenting-government-business%3A-the-dirks-manual [accessed 10 January 2020].

Duranti, L. (ed.) (2005) *The Long-Term Preservation of Authentic Electronic Records: findings of the InterPARES Project*, Archilab, www.interpares.org/book/index.cfm [accessed 11 February 2013].

Duranti, L. and Rogers, D. (eds) (2019) *Trusting Records in the Cloud*, Facet Publishing.

Evans, L. (2018) Language, Translation and Accounting: towards a critical research agenda, *Accounting, Auditing and Accountability Journal*, **31** (7), 1844–73.

FOLDOC (Free On-Line Dictionary of Computing) (2002) 'Record', http://foldoc.org/record [accessed 30 May 2013].

Flinn, A. (2011) Archival Activism: independent and community-led archives, radical public history and the heritage professions, *InterActions: UCLA Journal of Education and Information Studies*, **7** (2), https://escholarship.org/uc/item/9pt2490x.pdf [accessed 5 February 2020].

Foscarini, F. (2009) *Function-Based Records Classification Systems: an exploratory study of records management practices in central banks*, PhD thesis, University of British Columbia.

Foscarini, F. (2012) Diplomatics and Genre Theory as Complementary Approaches, *Archival Science*, **12** (4), 389–409.

Geertz, C. (1983) *Local Knowledge*, Basic Books.

Hofstede, G. (2001) *Culture's Consequences: comparing values, behaviors, institutions, and organizations across nations*, 2nd edn, Sage Publications.

House, J. (2003) English as a Lingua Franca: a threat to multilingualism? *Journal of Sociolinguistics*, **7** (4), 556–78.

International Organization for Standardization (ISO) (2016) ISO15489-1:2016 Information and documentation – Records management. Part 1: General.

InterPARES Project (n.d.) www.interpares.org [accessed 23 January 2013].

InterPARES 2 Terminology Database (n.d.) www.interpares.org/ip2/ip2_terminology_db.cfm [accessed 28 February 2013].

Karahanna, E., Evaristo, J.R. and Srite, M. (2005) Levels of Culture and Individual Behavior: an integrative perspective, *Journal of Global Information Management*, **13** (2), 1–20.

Lee, J. A. (2019) In Critical Condition: (un)becoming bodies in archival acts of truth telling, *Archivaria* **88**, 162–95.

MacNeil, H. (2000) *Trusting Records: legal, historical, and diplomatic perspectives*, Kluwer Academic Publishers.

META (Multilingual Europe Technology Alliance) (n.d.) The Swedish Language in the Digital Age – Executive Summary, www.meta-net.eu/whitepapers/volumes/swedish-executive-summary-en [accessed 2 May 2013].

Nestor (2008) Nestor-Kriterien: Kriterienkatalog vertrauenswürdige digitale Langzeitarchive, http://files.d-nb.de/nestor/materialien/nestor_mat_08.pdf [accessed 23 January 2013].

Oliver, G., Chawner, B. and Liu, H. (2011) Implementing Digital Archives: Issues of trust, *Archival Science*, **11**, 311–27.

Ramirez, M. H. (2015) Being Presumed Not to Be: a critique of whiteness as an archival imperative, *American Archivist*, **78** (2), 339–56.

RIMPA (2010) *Statement of Ethical Practice*, www.rimpa.com.au/assets/2011/03/StatementEthicalPractice.pdf [accessed 23 January 2013].

RLG (2002) *Trusted Digital Repositories: attributes and responsibilities. An OCLC-RLG report*, www.oclc.org/resources/research/activities/trustedrep/repositories.pdf [accessed 23 January 2013].

Schön, D. A. (1983) *The Reflective Practitioner: how professionals think in action*, Basic Books.

Smart, G. (2006) *Writing the Economy: activity, genre and technology in the world of banking*, Equinox.

Wickham, M. S. (2010) Reflective Practice and Mentoring in the Development of Archivists and Records Managers, *Comma*, **2010** (1), 123–39.

PART 6

CHAPTER 9

The toolkit

The Information Culture Analysis Toolkit (hereafter, the toolkit) that is introduced in this chapter is one of the most significant innovations produced by our research on information and recordkeeping culture. The toolkit was developed thanks to funding provided by the International Council on Archives' (ICA) Programme Commission (PCOM), which allowed us to conduct a series of case studies where we applied the ICF as presented in the first edition of this book (Oliver and Foscarini, 2014).

The chapter starts with an overview of the ICA-funded research project that resulted in the development of the toolkit as its major deliverable. The components of the toolkit and how they can be applied to a variety of recordkeeping environments will be described. This initial section is followed by a detailed explanation of the cultural indicators identified as key to the analysis of information culture – i.e. genres, workarounds and infrastructure. A brief discussion of the results of testing the toolkit in real organisations is followed by an explanation of the kind of reasoning that informs our culturally sensitive approach to information management and recordkeeping, that is, 'soft' systems thinking.

'Learning to walk the talk'

Immediately after the publication of *Records Management and Information Culture: tackling the people problem* (Oliver and Foscarini, 2014) we were awarded an ICA-PCOM grant that allowed us to carry out an action research project, 'Learning to Walk the Talk: Analysing Information Culture'. Through an exploration of the information cultures of archival authorities, the project aimed to help organisational actors to understand and apply the key concepts of information culture as part of next-generation recordkeeping practice. The decision to focus on archival authorities (namely, the national archives of

Australia, Fiji, the Netherlands and Brazil) had nothing to do with their core functions, in the sense that we were not interested in analysing the ways they managed their holdings or how they served researchers and the general public. Instead we wanted to study the information culture of communities (archivists and records managers) in different parts of the world that supposedly understand the value of records and are therefore expected to act accordingly ('walk the talk'). The ICF (Oliver and Foscarini, 2014) was used to guide our analysis; and the analysis was in turn used to test and improve the ICF – hence the modified framework presented in this book – as well as to create tools that would facilitate the application of the framework and its underlying concepts by anyone in the organisation.

The toolkit includes the following components:

- a data collection protocol
- an interview guide
- a data analysis template
- an information profile template.

The toolkit components have been translated into several languages, including French, Spanish, Portuguese and Korean, and a community of people sharing an interest in information culture was established on LinkedIn.[1]

Data collection protocol

This toolkit component has been designed as an *aide-mémoire* for those who plan to investigate the information and recordkeeping cultures of their own workplace and would like to be reminded of the basics of the ethnographic approach we recommend throughout this book (see especially Chapter 8). Before you start engaging with the on-site research process that will eventually result in an overview of the information/recordkeeping cultures characterising your organisation, or the group of people you work with, read this protocol to yourself and put on the 'ethnographer's hat'.

Data collection protocol

The best way to build a picture of an organisation's information culture is by talking to people, either by having one-on-one conversations or by having group discussions. Which you choose to do will vary according to the organisation and the relationship between staff. Group discussions can be

---

very productive and mean that you can talk to several people at once, but, if staff are likely to be reluctant to disagree with senior colleagues, then having meetings with individuals will be more productive.

The purpose of these conversations is not to check up on whether or not 'best practice' is being followed, but to find out how people actually go about using and managing information in their daily work, and what issues and challenges they meet. Provide reassurance that this is not an inspection or an audit.

Practicalities:

- Before visiting the organisation, do as much background reading as you can to familiarise yourself with its development, structure, mission and functions.
- Find out who can assist you in scheduling meetings, and provide them with enough information as possible about your objectives, to help prepare people to answer your questions.
- If possible, begin your visit by giving a presentation to as many of the staff as practical to explain the information culture concept and the purpose of the interviews.
- Try to talk to at least one person from each functional area. Ask each individual at the conclusion of the interview whether they can suggest anyone else whom you should talk to.
- Try to make sure that you don't just speak to people from the same level of the organisation.
- If the organisation is distributed (e.g. has a head office and regional branches), always try to talk to a sample of people in different locations. Views from head office and branches can be polar opposites; and particularly if ICT does not support collaborative working across the whole organisation, branch offices may establish very comprehensive 'shadow' systems and workarounds.
- The key skill in this type of interviewing is listening. Encourage the interviewee to be expansive in their responses, and be alert for relevant areas about which to ask for further information.

Interview guide

As discussed in Chapter 2, an interview guide is not meant to include any comprehensive or fixed sets of questions that should be asked in a certain order and without any divergence. On the contrary, this a flexible, expandable tool, consisting of indicative questions, that should act as a reminder for the interviewer of the areas that need to be covered, and that should allow for digressions and free flows of thoughts. Interviewees should feel comfortable answering your questions. Although you may not be required by your organisational policy to collect formal consent, it is important to provide interviewees with a safe space where they can express their views.

Interview guide

Consent procedure: Before starting with the interview, let your interviewee know how you are going to use the information they will provide, and emphasise the fact that there is no obligation for them to answer any of your questions, and they can withdraw their consent to use their information at any time.

Most of these questions should be regarded as starting points. Where appropriate, always follow up by exploring why. Understanding the 'why' holds the key to information culture:

1 **Please tell me about your role and your responsibilities**
   Always begin by asking people to explain their position in the organisation. This will give you the context you need to follow up and explore specific areas where necessary.

2 **How long have you worked in that position/for the organisation?**
   This information will help you to know the level of organisational knowledge the interviewee brings to the conversation. If someone has worked in a place for a long time they can be very useful in providing historical context; if they are new it is a good opportunity to learn how a relative outsider experiences the organisation.

3 **If you were to leave your current role/the organisation, what would you have to do to ensure the person who takes over from you would have all the information at their fingertips that they needed to do their job?**
   Responses to this question should give you insight into their everyday personal information management practices, and into their awareness of what they should be doing, but are not.

4 **Thinking about information, and finding out how things have been done and why decisions have been made, is there any particular advice you would give to your successor?**
   Responses may indicate whether there is reliance on individuals as sources of knowledge, or whether internal information systems are regarded as reliable and trustworthy.

---

5   Are you aware of the policies/guidelines you are supposed to follow with regard to information, and if so, are they realistic?

6   Are there any particular challenges that you face in working with information?

7   Are there any systems or processes relating to information that are particularly effective, or that work well?

8   Are there any particular features of the ICT infrastructure that you would like to comment on?

9   Do you (or your team) have any personal information systems or procedures that you've developed to help you work more effectively? Workarounds may be mentioned in answers to other questions, but in case they are not, this question asks about them specifically. It is very important to encourage people to talk about their unofficial ways of working, as these tell us a lot about information culture. An example of a workaround is keeping one's own paper working files.

10 Are there any particular document types (these could be anything, ranging from standardised forms used for reporting, to e-mails) that you think are characteristic of this workplace? Another way of asking about genres might be by talking about language usages, or special terms that are recurrently used in the organisation in some specific sense that is known only to insiders. Possible questions might be: 'What do you mean by …?'; 'Do you have some special way of calling …?'; 'I heard you saying "…". Can you explain that to me?'

11 Are there any particular meetings that regularly take place that influence information flow or information practices? This and the previous question are both specifically asking about genres. Both document types and meetings may have been mentioned in earlier responses, but, if not, these two questions target them specifically. Once they are identified, you can make direct reference to these genres in subsequent interviews. For example, 'tell me more about the blue cards. Do you use them?' or 'Can you access the minutes of the monthly managers' meetings?' With reference to meetings, possible sub-questions may be: 'Do you like the way in which [a specific type of meetings] is organised?'; 'Do you find these meetings useful?'; 'If so, to whom (managers, employees, …)?'

12a Can you tell me which of these terms (or any others) represent your workplace (department/office) best? Trust

Transparency
Openness
Indifference
Sloppiness
Accuracy
Customer orientation
Competitiveness
Relaxation
Pride
Professionalism
Solidarity
Secrecy
Team spirit
Positive attitude towards criticism
Compliance

12b Thinking about the whole organisation, would you apply the same terms?

13 How would you describe the organisational culture here?

Data analysis template

This toolkit component is based on the three cultural indicators – genres, workarounds and infrastructure – that we have identified as key to organise the data you will have collected through your interviews into manageable sub-sets, each pointing to some of the features included in the ICF. The meaning of genres, workarounds and infrastructure, and how these categories are supposed to be used in this context, will be further explained in the next sections of this chapter. Here, we will just emphasise that this way of categorising your interview data is meant to help you map your findings with the ICF levels, as a first step to build an information profile for your organisation or community, which is the main goal of this whole exercise.

Data analysis template

NB: There is inevitable overlap between the three broad categories of genres, workarounds and infrastructure. The important thing is to note information in one or another of these categories (or cultural indicators) – there is no need to repeat it unless thinking of it from a different perspective highlights different dimensions of information culture.

---

1   Genres
- What are the main/distinctive genres that get talked about? (NB: comprehensive list not necessary)
- What, where, how and why are they used; who uses them?
- Analysis: What do the genres tell us about the information culture?

2   Workarounds
- What unofficial systems and/or tools do people use?
- Why?
- What's the impact of these workarounds? Can they/should they be further developed?
- Analysis: What insight into information culture do these workarounds provide?

3   Infrastructure
- What formal systems/tools/resources exist to manage information (e.g. filing system, EDRMS, policies, laws, IT infrastructure)?
- Analysis: What does the infrastructure tell us about information culture?

Information profile template

The information profile is the final product of your information culture investigation. You should be sharing it with anyone interested, perhaps through a workshop or a series of workshops involving different groups within your organisation. It is important that you do not present it as an audit or a consultancy report. Rather, the information profile should be used as a tool to engage individuals – even those with very little or no interest in the subject matter – in an open and frank conversation about workplace strengths and weaknesses, and conforming and idiosyncratic behaviours when it comes to information management and recordkeeping. In other words, the purpose of this whole exercise is not to assess how well or badly the study participants manage their records, or how well the institution complies with recordkeeping best practice. Your aim should be to offer a 'rich picture' of the situation, which could be used to identify gaps and provide recommendations for improvement.

[Name of agency]: Information profile

This information profile has been developed from interviews conducted at [name] in [date], supplemented by information publicly available from websites, such as [...]. It begins by providing a brief background to the current environment, and then reports observations from the perspective of the three levels of the information culture model.

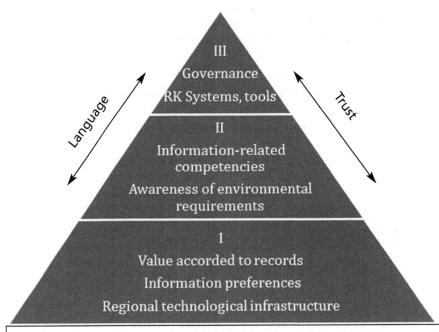

Background

[*Overview of context, with a focus on key issues such as major projects that the agency is involved with.*]

To gain an overview of the values of the organisation, interviewees were asked to select from a list of words those that best characterised their specific workplaces [*summary of responses, noting any differences between values assigned to team and those attributed to organisation as a whole*].

Level one observations

Features observed at this level are fundamental influences impacting on the ways in which information is managed. They may not be possible to change, but must be clearly identified in order to develop strategies and solutions that are appropriate to the context. The factors to be taken into consideration at this level are as follows:

- the value (or respect) accorded to information of different types, with particular focus on records. This will include recognition and awareness of the need to manage certain information for the purposes of accountability, as well as for the purposes of facilitating knowledge and awareness;

- preferences for different communication media and formats, as well as preferences with regard to sharing information. The former involves consideration of preferred primary sources for information; the latter, the level of granularity to which information sharing is regarded as the norm by employees;
- regional technological infrastructure. The technological infrastructure in the country or region where the organisation is located.

Value accorded to records
Information preferences
Information flows
Regional IT infrastructure

Level two observations

The second level of the pyramid represents the skills, knowledge and expertise of employees relating to information management, which can be acquired and/or extended in the workplace. This is placed in the middle of the triangle because training development will take into account those fundamental influences at the bottom. The skills, knowledge and expertise can be divided into two broad categories:

- information-related competencies, including information and digital literacy
- awareness of environmental (societal and organisational) requirements relating to recordkeeping.

Information-related competencies
Awareness of societal/organisational requirements

Level three observations

At the tip of the pyramid are two organisational features which are highly significant for successful recordkeeping and are the most susceptible to change. These two features are:

- the information governance model that is in place in the organisation, as reflected in the organisation's information technology infrastructure
- the organisational recordkeeping systems and tools.

Information governance
Recordkeeping systems and tools

Metalevels

Metalevels may apply to any of the features included in the pyramid. The metalevel factors are:

- the language people use when talking about the way they manage information; what happens when multiple languages (as different mother tongues or different jargons) are used and one of them becomes dominant;
- the trust people have in existing recordkeeping systems, practices, and dedicated units.

Language
Trust

Last words

[*Use this section for any overall observations summing up the overall information culture, and to provide recommendations, as appropriate.*]

Genres

As we have seen throughout this book, the recordkeeping culture of any organised group of people – that is, their shared values and attitudes towards information as evidence – can be explored by observing how people act together. Actions and transactions may be carried out through gestures (e.g. handshakes), oral utterances (e.g. 'I agree'), written records (e.g. contracts), information systems (e.g. travel booking platforms) and other recognisable communication tools that work for the social group we are observing. When organisations and communities enact the same forms of communication over and over again to accomplish their goals, we can start identifying their 'genres'.

In a ground-breaking article published in 1984 American communication scholar Carolyn Miller defined genres as 'typified rhetorical actions based in recurrent situations' (Miller, 1984, 159). Miller's focus on everyday, non-literary forms of communication, and her insistence on the 'social action' performed by genres, revolutionised the field of genre studies, which was until then primarily interested in classic forms of rhetorical discourse and theories of classification of literary texts. Rhetorical Genre Studies (RGS) developed as a branch of research having among its purposes that of shedding light on how people use genres – including 'genres of organisational communication', that is, invoices, business letters, memoranda, project progress reports, contracts, etc. (Yates and Orlikowski, 1992) – to shape the environment in which they act, and how the genres they use contribute, in turn, to shaping who they are as a social group (Artemeva and Freedman, 2008). It is therefore evident that a study of the genres typically enacted in a certain organisational context can be revealing of its cultural characteristics, including the recordkeeping culture.

The contributions made by RGS to the concept of a record and the traditional understanding of the record's form and function have been discussed by Fiorella (Foscarini, 2012; 2013; 2015), while Gillian has explored the potential of genre ideas for digital recordkeeping, with particular regard to the appraisal of digital records (Oliver et al., 2008). Here we want to emphasise that genres, as socially recognised communication patterns, embed and reveal the information culture of a workplace.

As demonstrated in previous chapters, it is by paying attention to the actual practices that people carry out in organisations (how they share/do not share information, what preferences they have in relation to media, how they collaborate when writing documents together, etc.) that we may get access to their information culture, as our attitudes and values towards information shape and are shaped by the kinds of information we create and use to accomplish our work. By analysing the 'recurrent situations' that prompt certain record types (or genres) and are at the same time the outcome of those 'typified responses' (Miller, 1984), we can get insights into both the context of records creation (not as an abstraction, but as a set of specific, historically and socially situated circumstances) and the formal and substantial characteristics of the created records.

The meeting genre

A genre of organisational communication that is rather pervasive in contemporary organisations is the meeting. As 'physical, social, and symbolic cultural tools' (Yates and Orlikowski, 1992), meetings play an instrumental role in shaping the character of an organisation. Also, the way they are enacted can tell us a lot about the values and attitudes of meeting participants. Schwartzman (1989) argued that 'meetings provide individuals with a way to make sense of as well as to legitimate what otherwise might seem to be disparate talk and action … [As such,] meetings are a form that frequently stabilises but can just as easily destabilise and transform a cultural system in ways that are often unrecognised and even unintended by actors in the system.' In RGS terms, we could say that meetings contribute to the 'normalisation' of practices that all organisations need in order to function: they support the 'centripetal impulse' that was mentioned in Chapter 7. At the same time, meetings may be sites of resistance and ad hoc innovation, i.e. they work as a 'centrifugal' force capable of transforming the organisation, its members and its genres (Spinuzzi 2003; Foscarini 2012).

Research conducted in 2015–16 thanks to the ICA's support revealed that in one of the case study sites people referred to three kinds of meetings, which they called 'weekly meetings', 'knowledge meetings' and 'strategic meetings'. It is important to pay attention to the ways organisational actors talk about their own genres, as this can help, as in this case, to identify 'sub-genres' within the broader meeting genre. Each of the three sub-genres appeared to have very specific characteristics and functions. 'Weekly meetings' were short, focused on one or two subjects at most and cross-departmental. All interviewees commented that they loved attending the weekly meetings, even when the subject was not directly relevant to their work, as they always learned something and there was a 'positive atmosphere' in the meetings. The same could be said about 'knowledge meetings', which were welcomed opportunities to share information on ongoing or just-completed projects and to give and get feedback on such projects. They were initiated by project leaders, and everyone in the organisation, independently of their rank or occupation, was invited to attend. Less inclusive, but still open to broad participation from different units, 'strategic meetings' happened more seldom and were used by managers to communicate decisions. Yet participants were allowed to make suggestions, and no one complained about the atmosphere in or the usefulness of strategic meetings. To the researcher's question about the records produced in relation to these three sub-genres (e.g. agendas, minutes, notes), most interviewees replied that they were not sure about official records or other formal ways of capturing what was discussed in these meetings, even in relation to the more official gatherings.

By applying the toolkit to these findings one can conclude that this organisation showed a strong focus on knowledge creation and knowledge sharing, preferably through informal means (ICF level one). Records did not play a key role in communication and their evidential value was under-estimated (ICF level one). Also, informal, spontaneous learning seemed to be considered more effective than formal education or training (ICF level two); and information flowed in all directions (ICF levels 1 and 3).

Workarounds

We discussed and provided examples of workarounds in Chapter 7 in the context of policy analysis, where we acknowledged that people often resort to unofficial, local practices in order to cope with the rigidity of official systems or the complexity of established rules. By sharing these workarounds with co-workers during daily enactments (e.g. spreadsheet used in an office to take note of incoming applications, when the official recordkeeping tool does not facilitate the provision of a summary overview of them and by continuing to rely on the spreadsheet over time, it sometimes happens that the workaround is institutionalised and becomes the new official practice (e.g. the recordkeeping tool is modified so as to integrate the functionality of the spreadsheet). To borrow a metaphor from urban design, we may say that workarounds are like cow-paths (also known as calf-paths or desire lines), the paths that pedestrians take informally over grassy areas, rather than using an established, usually paved route. These cow-paths are people's chosen ways of navigating space, emerging first as barely noticeable tracks that eventually turn into beaten paths through recurring use. Records professionals tend to overlook or disregard these unofficial practices which result directly from the preferences, desires or needs of organisational actors, and to focus on the documentary paved roads designed by IT specialists, information engineers and business managers. As a result, official systems (e.g. EDRMS) end up capturing only the 'best records' that comply with system demands, not the imperfect records created outside of any official frameworks and which would be great evidence of how the process is actually carried out.

According to RGS, genres are always 'stabilised-for-now or stabilised-enough sites of social and ideological action' (Schryer, 1993, 200). This means that change is part of their nature – as the dynamic view of records and archives involved in the records continuum model suggests as well. What is new and interesting about the genre approach is the recognition that genre/record transformation is an outcome of the continuous negotiations that take place when individuals interact, mainly through exchanges of spoken and written texts, in order to carry out their work. As mentioned in Chapter 8, the language used by records professionals (our jargon), with all its ambiguity and difficulty, is the always-in-flux result of such negotiations of meaning. Looking at recordkeeping through a genre lens is a way of importing the social and rhetorical dimensions of communication into our discourse, thus acknowledging that making, receiving, organising, accessing, maintaining and destroying records are actions that do not happen in a vacuum. They are social actions that reflect who we are, what we believe in and how we want to position ourselves and the records we create and manage in relation to anyone else and any other existing records.

Infrastructure

As an information culture indicator, infrastructure refers to all material and immaterial (e.g. political, economic, legal, technological, architectural, geographical) frameworks that characterise a specific workplace or a situation. Obviously, providing fully comprehensive analyses of the infrastructure might not be possible. In some cases the researcher will mainly focus on the regional technological infrastructure affecting a certain organisation (see Chapter 4); in other cases the legal and regulatory infrastructure within which the organisation operates will be investigated (see Chapter 6); and so on. As mentioned earlier in this book (see in particular Chapter 2, where we discussed the basic ideas involved in the theory of structuration [Giddens, 1984]), the 'invisible infrastructures' that we build to allow our living in society, and that we continuously maintain, negotiate and redefine, become visible in those moments when the circumstances of our 'acting together' (Miller, 1984) change. Shifts in perceived needs among the general public, the release of a new piece of technology, etc. may make us feel that the current legislation is inadequate, current technologies do not do what they are supposed to do, etc. As a researcher of recordkeeping cultures you will realise that some particular infrastructure calls for your attention more than any others when people talk about it, complain about its unnecessary constraints or praise it as a great enabler for their actions.

In one of the ICA-funded case studies involving archival institutions which we conducted in 2015–16, we noticed a striking difference between the ICT infrastructure in place for the management of the institution's archival holdings and that devoted to the management of its current records. It was evident that the archival institution in question did not value its internal recordkeeping and invested all of its resources into its outward-looking activities, which mostly concerned the online availability of its collections. People in the organisation were aware of the inadequacy of their EDRMS, which was consistently described as slow, outdated and insufficiently integrated with other applications; however, this two-speed infrastructure (an accelerated technological solution for the historical material, and a slow one for 'the archive of the Archives', as the EDRMS was called within the institution) was hardly addressed. The information culture study was an opportunity for all actors involved (records managers, archivists, directors of information management units, directors of collection management units, IT specialists, project managers and consultants) to confront this issue, and to do so in a structured way thanks to the instruments provided by the ICF.

Trialling the toolkit

The information culture analysis toolkit was tested (independently of the ICF developers) by records professionals working for two Australasian universities in 2016. One of the key lessons learned from this pilot study was that 'the effectiveness of the information culture toolkit to analyse people's values and attitudes towards information rests on the records managers' ability to approach their subjects with ethnographic sensitivity' (Oliver et al., 2018, 178). In Chapter 8 we explained how to be an 'ethnographer' in your own workplace. Here we want to restate that the toolkit itself can and should be used as a vehicle to foster an open dialogue among all parties involved in the investigation of their recordkeeping culture.

As mentioned above, the infrastructure within which people develop their work routines, as well as the official and unofficial genres (or workarounds) that are the substance of such routines, may be invisible to the organisation's members. By using the toolkit as a device to structure a conversation on the importance which people attach to their records, on their feelings towards the information systems in place, on the discrepancies between prescribed and actual information practices, etc., the records professionals – who acted as ethnographers within their own workplace – were able to bring to light issues that would otherwise never have been discussed, as they would be considered an unavoidable fact of life, something which no one could do anything about. As the researchers reported:

> One of the unanticipated benefits of using the toolkit was that some directors, who would normally show no interest in recordkeeping issues, were eager to learn about the information culture of their units. In particular, they wanted to know how their local information culture may affect – in both positive and negative ways – the overall organisational performance.
>
> (Oliver et al., 2018, 181)

Soft systems thinking

The suggestion that the toolkit, and the information culture approach overall, can be used as a 'dialogic tool', as a way of bringing to the table an open discussion on issues that touch every individual in the organisation (as everyone is a records creator), as a tool to build relationships among the members of a community, is also part of the message involved in *soft systems thinking*. In this section, we review the origins and main characteristics of Soft Systems Methodology (SSM), which is a research design approach relying on soft systems reasoning.

One of the key thoughts that in the mid-1960s inspired some professors of systems engineering at Lancaster University in the UK to develop SSM was that 'human situations in which people were attempting to take purposeful action which were meaningful for them' (i.e. one of the definitions of 'human activity systems' suggested by Checkland, 1999, A7) are more complex, less structured and less easily definable than the natural and mathematical systems investigated by the 'hard' sciences. Trying to apply engineering-like methods (e.g. model building, cost-benefit analysis) to, for instance, management issues (e.g. decision-making processes, conflict resolution), as their contemporaries had been doing (see Simon, 1976), was to their eyes inadequate, and would result in ineffective solutions, for the very reason that human beings play a major role in the 'problem situation' that needs to be resolved.

Due to different life experiences, educational and professional backgrounds, and any other pre-existing social, economic and cultural factors, each individual necessarily has a very specific way of looking at his or her world – Checkland (1999) uses the term 'Weltanschauung' – and this will influence his or her understanding of what the problem is:

> A problem relating to real-world manifestations of human activity systems is a condition characterized by a sense of mismatch, which eludes precise definition, between what is perceived to be actuality and what is perceived might become actuality.
>
> (Checkland, 1999, 155)

Drawing *a rich picture* of the problem situation, a picture that takes into consideration as many viewpoints as possible and does not privilege one perspective over another, is the first step involved in SSM (Checkland, 1999, 165–6). If, for instance, e-mail management is a problem in your workplace (and where it is not?), you will seek the opinions not only of information professionals but also of lawyers, accountants, human resources experts and anyone concerned in the problem situation identified. Their particular interpretations of why e-mails are not managed properly will be matched with information about their respective worldviews.

Exploring the problem situation and finding out what people think about it should actually be seen as an ongoing activity. Describing such enquiry into the 'real world' as an initial step makes explaining the SSM approach easier; each 'part' of the methodology can be a starting point and can be repeated as many times as needed. Another methodological tip concerns the way of communicating your objectives and representing your findings. Checkland

and colleagues recommend using pictures (simple graphic elements such as oval shapes and curved lines) rather than words, as 'pictures are a better medium than linear prose for expressing relationships' (Checkland, 1999, A16). However, as discussed in Chapter 3, not everyone appreciates visual representations in the same way; so if you and your interlocutor feel more comfortable using words, feel free to do so.

To allow for the interpretation and evaluation of your findings, the data collected must be translated into multiple *'conceptual models'*. We will not elaborate here on the technical aspects involved in SSM model building (Checkland, 1999, 169–76; Checkland and Scholes, 1999). We will just emphasise that in a 'soft' systems thinking approach models are conceived very differently from the way they are understood and operationalised in 'hard' systems thinking domains. First of all, SSM encourages you to build, and pay equal attention to, not just one but as many 'relevant systems' as there are definitions of the problem situation you are tackling. Second, models in SSM are supposed to be 'accounts of concepts of pure purposeful activity, based on declared world-views' (Checkland, 1999, A21); as such, they might not be representing anything 'real' in the outside world. The purpose of building formal models from those subjective views or individual projections is to enable a *'structured discussion'* among all interested parties about the situation that is perceived as problematic (Checkland, 1999, 177–80).

The goal of this debate, during which the models are compared with one another and with real-world happenings, is neither to find a 'solution' to the problem at stake nor to bring any of the models to perfection (as is the case, for instance, in engineering). The goal is to identify actions that are considered suitable from the point of view of the overall logic of the system ('systemically desirable') and in line with the characteristics of the organisation, the people in it and their shared experiences ('culturally feasible') in order to improve the situation (Checkland, 1999, 180–3). Rather than the implementation of a new system or policy, the actions agreed on might simply consist in a change of attitude or the acquisition of new awareness that might materialise in 'accommodations' to alleviate existing conditions.

Because people's perceptions of problems are doomed to change with time, and any actions to improve the situation will necessarily generate new problems, SSM as a structured, rigorous approach to investigating our subjective world is, in principle, an ongoing, never-ending process. As Figure 9.1 on the next page shows, the basic 'parts' constituting SSM may be represented as iterative components of a learning cycle. Where to start and how to proceed depend on the objectives of the user of the methodology, the resources available and any other relevant constraints.

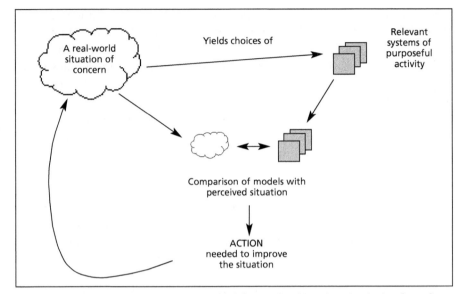

Figure 9.1 *SSM learning cycle. Adapted from Checkland and Scholes (1999), Figure 1.3, p. 7.* Reproduced with permission.

As pointed out elsewhere (Foscarini, 2010), records professionals may benefit in many ways from the (partial or complete) application of SSM as an 'organised learning system' (Checkland, 1999, A8). SSM can teach them how to 'read' a complex situation from different angles, how to evaluate various emerging ideas (some of which might be totally unanticipated) based on people's expectations, intellectual positions and prejudices, as well as how to achieve some agreeable compromise that would satisfy both their and their users' interests. The standards, models and paradigms we have been using throughout this book (from ISO15489 to DIRKS and the records continuum) are extremely important reference points for our profession. However, one of the lessons of SSM is that they are not unquestionable laws that fit each and every environment. Their 'desirability' and 'feasibility' will have to be checked against other models based on different, situated perceptions of the reality. By being open to new perspectives and adapting our established professional tools accordingly, we might end up with records management configurations that somehow deviate from the 'canon' but will be better embraced and supported by our local communities.

Summary and conclusions

The main goal of this chapter has been to describe the components of the information culture analysis toolkit that was developed as an outcome of a series of case studies where the initial instantiation of the ICF was used and tested. The application of the toolkit should facilitate the capture and processing of the great amount of data that every study of this kind tends to produce.

The key cultural indicators labelled as genres, workarounds and infrastructure were explained in some detail, and are connected to the soft systems thinking approach that we consider essential to any culturally sensitive research endeavour.

Note

1 https://www.linkedin.com/groups/4448140/.

References

Artemeva, N. and Freedman, A. (eds) (2008) *Rhetorical genre studies and beyond.* Inkshed Publications.

Checkland, P. (1999) *System thinking, system practice.* Chichester, UK: John Wiley & Sons Ltd.

Checkland, P. and Scholes, J. (1999) *Soft Systems Methodology in Action*, John Wiley & Sons Ltd.

Foscarini, F. (2010) Understanding the Context of Records Creation and Use: 'Hard' versus 'soft' approaches to records management, *Archival Science*, **10**, 389–407.

Foscarini, F. (2012) Diplomatics and Genre Theory as Complementary Approaches, *Archival Science*, **12** (4), 389–409.

Foscarini, F. (2013) Record as Social Action: understanding organizational records through the lens of genre theory. *Information Research* **18** (3) – paper C08 http://InformationR.net/ir/18-3/colis/paperC08.html [accessed 30 January 2020].

Foscarini, F. (2015) Organizational Records as Genres. An analysis of the 'documentary reality' of organizations from the perspectives of diplomatics, records management and rhetorical genre studies. In: Andersen, J. (ed.), *Genre Theory in Information Studies*, Emerald, 115–32.

Giddens, A. (1984) *The Constitution of Society: outline of the theory of structuration*, University of California Press.

Miller, C. R. (1984) Genre as Social Action, *Quarterly Journal of Speech*, **70** (2), 151–67.

Oliver, G. and Foscarini, F. (2014) *Records Management and Information Culture: tackling the people problem*, Facet Publishing.

Oliver, G., Kim, Y. and Ross, S. (2008) Documentary Genre and Digital Recordkeeping: red herring or a way forward? *Archival Science*, **8** (4), 295–305.

Oliver, G., Foscarini, F., Sinclair, C., Nicholls, C. and Loriente, L. (2018) Ethnographic Sensitivity and Current Recordkeeping: applying information culture analysis in the workplace, *Records Management Journal*, **28** (2), 175–86.

Schwartzman, H. B. (1989) *The Meeting: gatherings in organizations and communities*, Plenum Press.

Simon, H. (1976) *Administrative Behavior*, 3rd edn, The Free Press.

Spinuzzi, C. (2003) *Tracing Genres through Organizations: a sociocultural approach to information design*, MIT Press.

Yates, J. and Orlikowski, W. J. (1992) Genres of Organizational Communication: a structuractional approach to studying communication and media, *Academy of Management Review*, **17** (2), 299–326.

PART 7

CHAPTER 10

Bringing it all together and moving forward

Recordkeepers are faced with enormous challenges: on the one hand, demonstrating their relevance in an information environment that is in a constant state of flux, while on the other attempting to just get on and do their job of managing information as evidence, for accountability purposes. The demands of one may mean that the other is neglected, or only partially addressed. Additionally, in their role as mediators between various subject area experts (who may have very different needs in terms of both evidence and information) and IT specialists (responsible for designing and maintaining the systems used to manage corporate information) records professionals occupy a rather uncomfortable position in organisations, one that requires not only disciplinary knowledge but also 'people skills'. The latter may be described as the ability to listen and to communicate effectively, thereby building relationships of trust and productive interactions with co-workers (Bolton, 1986). Taking an information culture perspective will assist in cultivating such 'soft skills', thus providing a very different view of the workplace and its challenges, which in turn can lead to more creative and innovative approaches to the problems we face.

The purpose of this final chapter is twofold: first, to provide an overview of assessment techniques that have been detailed throughout the book and to consolidate the next steps suggestions for subsequent actions; and second, to consider how information culture perspectives can be included in archives and records education and training courses.

Assessment techniques

As discussed in Chapter 1, the development of new tools, standards and approaches is increasingly being trumpeted. However, the downside is that some seem to be represented as universal cure-alls, and figuring out where and when to apply them is left to the users of these new tools. As seen in

Chapter 9, taking a 'soft' systems thinking approach may help. Another useful consideration is that existing and future methodologies for calculating metrics, such as the various maturity models and impact calculators, should be used judiciously as part of a suite of tools. We need to be able to assess when, where and how each of these is best used; if a particular approach is going to be most effective in terms of communicating to management, then that could be a very valid reason for using it. Our information culture assessment can be supplemented by using other metrics, but these cannot replace taking an information culture perspective. Table 10.1 suggests where data collected with existing tools is most relevant for supplementing information culture analysis.

Table 10.1 *Contribution of existing tools to information culture analysis*

Existing tool	ICF level	Characteristic	Contribution of tool
RM Maturity Model	One	Values accorded to records (records management infrastructure)	May assist in communicating with management
DIRKS Step C	Two	Awareness of recordkeeping requirements	Helps to determine what those requirements are
DIRKS Step H	Metalevel	Trust in systems	Provides evidence of the trustworthiness of systems; Supports good public relations

Applying an ICF and mindset to recordkeeping in organisations will help not only in understanding the local and surrounding environment but also in working out contextually appropriate strategies, policies and processes. A number of different assessment techniques have been identified throughout this book; Table 10.2 brings them all together and indicates which ICF level and characteristic they can be used for and their ease of application (on a scale of 1–5, with 1 being the easiest and least resource intensive).

Table 10.2 *Summary of assessment techniques and their characteristics, including relevant ease of use*

Type of technique	Technique	Level	Characteristic	Ease of application
Engaging with people	Survey	One	Values accorded to records (attitudes and behaviours)	4
		One	Information preferences (limited to identifying possible national culture characteristics)	4
		One	Regional technological infrastructure (risks of electronic communications)	5
		Two	Information-related competencies	4
		Two	Awareness of recordkeeping requirements	4
		Metalevel	Trust in recordkeeping systems	4
		Metalevel	Language (local and rhetorical uses)	5
	Conducting interviews	One	Values accorded to records (attitudes and behaviours)	5
		One	Values accorded to records (IT usage)	5
		One	Regional technological infrastructure (risks of electronic communications)	5
		Two	Information-related competencies	5
		Two	Awareness of recordkeeping requirements	5
		Metalevel	Language (local uses and rhetoric)	5
		Metalevel	Trust in recordkeeping systems	5

Continued

Table 10.2 *Continued*

Type of technique	Technique	Level	Characteristic	Ease of application
Engaging with people	Profiling	Three	Corporate IT governance	3
	Ethnography	Metalevel	Language (local and rhetorical uses)	5
		Metalevel	Trust in recordkeeping systems	2–5 (depending on the extent of activity involved)
Desk research	Documentary analysis	One	Values accorded to records (records management infrastructure)	1
		One	Values accorded to records (attitudes and behaviours)	1
		One	Information preferences (information sharing)	2
		Metalevel	Language (local uses and rhetoric)	2
		One	Regional technological infrastructure (technical reports)	1
		Three	Corporate IT governance	2
	Observation	One	Values accorded to records (records management infrastructure)	1
	Transaction log analysis	One	Values accorded to records (IT usage)	1–3 (depending on ease of access to data logs)
		One	Information preferences	1–3

Continued

Table 10.2 *Continued*

Type of technique	Technique	Level	Characteristic	Ease of application
Desk research	Self-assessment of skills required by records management function	Two	Information-related competencies	3
	Determining national cultural dimensions	One	Information preferences	1

Interventions

A wide range of approaches have been suggested for follow-up after data collection and analysis. These are summarised in Table 10.3.

Table 10.3 *Summary of next steps suggestions, including their respective purposes*

	ICF Level	Characteristic	Why?
Speak their language	One	Values accorded to records	Critical when there is little fundamental understanding of or respect for records and recordkeeping
Be open to new approaches	One	Values accorded to records	Critical when there is little fundamental understanding of or respect for records and recordkeeping
	One	Information preferences	To ensure that plurality of information preferences are addressed
Customise marketing to take into account user characteristics	One	Information preferences	To prioritise features of recordkeeping systems that correspond with users' information preferences

Continued

Table 10.3 *Continued*

	ICF Level	Characteristic	Why?
Develop dictionaries of local definitions of terms	Metalevel	Language considerations	To facilitate communication and understanding
Participate in projects for the design of the internet of the future	One	Regional technological infrastructure	To facilitate harmonised approach and include records-related concerns
Work collaboratively with colleagues in IT and HR	Two	Information-related competencies	To determine information literacy/digital literacy profiles for staff
Determine appropriate training delivery modes and policies	Two	Information-related competencies and awareness of recordkeeping requirements	To ensure range of learning styles taken into account; to minimise barriers to learning
Build relationships with IT	Three	Corporate IT governance	To influence decision making
Be a reflective practitioner	Metalevel	Trust in recordkeeping systems	To ensure ongoing sensitivity and responsiveness to information culture features

The need for training and education

In this book we have attempted to present our research and ideas about recordkeeping culture in a way that will facilitate their uptake by professional recordkeepers in their practice. However, the concepts addressed are complex and often quite at odds with more traditional approaches to recordkeeping. Furthermore, although we have made every effort to package our content so that it can easily be applied, we are under no illusion of effecting meaningful change in the attitudes and perspectives of the recordkeeping professions simply by writing a book. Thus we decided that it would be most appropriate to devote the final section of this book to training and education needs, as this is where deeper, more influential change can be initiated.

The central focus of recordkeeping education and training programmes is generally on an information artefact, the record, and on recordkeeping best practice. Emphasising and foregrounding human factors can be difficult to do, and if they are addressed at all they are unlikely to be embedded throughout teaching and learning. To really influence change, a shift in emphasis needs to occur, and cultural awareness needs to be incorporated into education and training for the profession. Therefore, an important component in our practice as educators has been to develop ways to deliver our content such that it will be meaningful and impactful, regardless of the geographic and social setting, and, most importantly, to accommodate the diversity of perspectives that we seek to recognise in recordkeeping cultures.

We have previously emphasised the importance of ethnographic sensitivity in recordkeeping practice (Oliver et al., 2018). In more traditional curricula for both current records management and archival science, consideration of the individuals involved is often reduced to nebulous and generic 'users', who may well be regarded as obstacles or hindrances to achieving respective missions. Formal educational programmes for professional qualifications should be the ideal time to start developing sensitivities to the diversity of people interacting with records and thus to equip new professionals with the insight necessary to understand socio-cultural settings and their implications for our disciplinary concerns. This applies to all students, regardless of their disciplinary background and future career aspirations as records managers or archivists. In this book we have concentrated on contemporary workplaces and community settings and this is reflected in the examples we have used. However, analysis of historical information cultures also has considerable potential for providing rich insight into today's recordkeeping problems and thus can contribute not only to practice change but also to theory. For some years Professor Eric Ketelaar has emphasised the importance of historical analysis for insight into the present, explaining that:

> Understanding the contingencies in the history of control through communication is important [because they ...] impact on the creation, maintenance and use of records. Such understanding may also contribute to our comprehension of current and future remediation, involving the adaptation and reorganisation of handed down technologies which affect recordkeeping and its social and cultural contexts.
>
> (Ketelaar, 2006)

More recently, he has written a rich and rewarding in-depth study of the social history of Dutch archives which focuses on the people involved (Ketelaar, 2020). We have also contributed to this canon with an analysis of particular cases in the 1930s in Italy, China and the Netherlands and consideration of what lessons we can draw for insight into contemporary environments (Foscarini et al., 2020), and we are keen to encourage more research into historical information cultures. We cannot emphasise enough the relevance of information culture to recordkeeping training and education, whether the disciplinary context is that of history or of information science.

We make a distinction between training and education. We use 'training' to refer to skill and knowledge development for existing practitioners, delivered in short, time-bound segments such as workshops and seminars. By 'education' we refer in-depth teaching and learning delivered as part of a professional qualification to students who are likely to be new to our discipline. The following two scenarios provide real-life examples of our attempts to address these issues.

Training for recordkeeping professionals

In conjunction with the development of the ICA toolkit (see Chapter 9) we ran a series of workshops at national archives around the world and at archives conferences. The challenge was to present totally new ways of thinking about longstanding issues and problems to existing, possibly senior, practitioners, and in so doing to influence change in their ways of thinking and doing. Resistance or refusal to listen may be inevitable if new ideas are presented in such a way as to suggest that existing ways of doing are wrong or inappropriate.

We were also conscious of the fact that those working at our national archival institutions are often regarded as authorities on the issues we were seeking to address, and might well already feel themselves to be under siege from constant criticism. We had to find a way of communicating that would not only motivate listening and engagement but also take into account potential cultural misunderstandings and language barriers. The solution we came up with involved the development of video animations.

Our two short video animations featured characters from two fictional archival authorities, the National Archives of Fantasyland and the National Archives of the Principality of Ruritania. Characters included the chief archivists and records managers of each institution, as well as other archivists. Carefully crafted short scripts were written for each character, emphasising that character's perspectives. So, for instance, while Daisy the Records

Manager laments her low status and complains that no one will listen to her at the National Archives of Ruritania, the Chief Archivist proclaims the organisation as one big happy family with a unified vision, world leading in all things digital. At the same time, Hetty the Archivist is happily totally immersed in the wonder of the treasures of the past, the paper records she is processing, and regards any recordkeeping requirement as a totally unnecessary diversion from her core mission. We also made sure that each character made at least one reference to simple examples of the diagnostic factors (genres, workarounds and infrastructure) described in Chapter 9.

These videos have been extremely well received and in every workshop encouraged participants to reflect on their own settings. Our main device to navigate resistance and to transcend cultural barriers and misunderstandings was the use of humour, and our deliberately exaggerated characters certainly did provoke a lot of laughter. Because we used minimalist scripts we were able to commission their translation into a number of different languages and either distribute the translated scripts where necessary or in one case were able to provide subtitles (in Spanish). Our experiences with developing these workshops has enabled us to suggest a set of key requirements for information culture training:

- Use a multiplicity of voices to illustrate conflicting and contradictory perspectives. Video animations are one example; another could be role-play scenarios.
- Use humour as much as possible to facilitate communication and to help navigate resistance to listening to what can be perceived as threats to established ways of thinking and doing.
- Provide examples of difficult concepts such as genres in ways that are relevant to participants' own experiences.
- Make text components concise and succinct. They should be delivered in participants' mother tongue wherever possible, or translated.

Education for recordkeeping students

A prerequisite for conveying the complexity and importance of information culture to the next generation of practitioners is an understanding of workplace realities. When delivering training we can work from the assumption that the participants will have at least some experience of the messiness and contradictory nature of human dynamics in the workplace. However, with students this experience cannot be assumed, so it is important not only to use plenty of real-life examples but also to try to develop a replica environment as a basis for discussion and assignments. Case studies are very useful as a means of illustrating problem areas and can be used as a basis for an in-depth replica environment.

At Monash University in Melbourne, Australia, the student cohort for a new postgraduate course on Recordkeeping Informatics was very large and very diverse. The students were not generally motivated by a desire to explore new approaches to recordkeeping theory or even to pursue recordkeeping as a career, but many were attracted by the absence of a formal examination. Most students had little or no work experience in any bureaucratic setting, so many examples that would normally be used to illustrate particular problems or issues were likely to be ineffective.

To address this a case study of a fictitious large Australian telecommunications company called ComTelDat was developed. Then, inspired by the success of the training videos described above, we attempted to bring the organisation to life by conducting 'interviews' with the key stakeholders. In this case the key stakeholders were the privacy officer, the enterprise architect, a business analyst, the cybersecurity manager, the data manager, the IT strategy manager, the records manager, the head of corporate services and, to provide an outside view, an external contractor. A short script was written for each character, and a variety of PhD students and colleagues were recruited to audio record each script. We wanted to make sure that the characters were as diverse as the students, so although all 'interviews' were in English our interviewees were of different ages and genders and had a range of accents.

The following are four examples of our scripts which show the conversational tone we aimed for and the articulation of very different perspectives on the same organisation:

1 *The Enterprise Architect*: 'My role as enterprise architect feels like mission impossible. In a nutshell, I'm leading a three-year project to identify the IT systems currently used by ComTelDat. It might sound straightforward, but let me tell you, it's anything but. Do you have any idea how big this place is, and how long it's been in existence? Then you've got all the chopping and changing about business direction, introducing new services one minute and canning them the next. It all adds up to a very, very complex organisation, which means there's a mare's nest of ICT systems to try to sort out. To start off with I thought this would be easy. I'm really systematic by nature so I constructed a project plan and thought I'll just work my way through each division, section and business unit. What I didn't realise until later on was that in

some divisions the business units have got real autonomy, they've got large budgets and purchasing power of their own so tend to respond to work pressures by buying systems and software to fix the problems, a real Band Aid approach to life. Have you heard about shadow IT? Sometimes I think there are more shadows in ComTelDat than substance! If and when I ever manage to get a handle on what IT systems ComTelDat has, that will give me the basis I need to develop corporate standards for purchase and maintenance, and what seems to be more improbable by the minute, a common vocabulary for the business. Nobody argues with the fact that our customers are our most valuable resource – but you wouldn't believe how many different ways there are of referring to customers in our systems – which means that we can't exchange data about them. If you've got an account with ComTelDat, chances are you'll be represented a zillion different ways in our systems, and none of them talk to each other. When you ring customer service about a problem with your mobile, don't expect them to know anything about the problems you've had for the last decade with your landline! And now of course everyone's dead scared of transgressing some privacy rule or other, so it's even more unlikely that we'll ever get systems talking to each other. The other big challenge is what I think of as the ComTelDat mindset. It's like a game, as soon as someone new appears (I started six months ago and it already feels like a lifetime) certain people seem to take great pleasure in giving them the run around. Ok, I know that what I'm doing has been attempted before, I've heard that so many times already. But what happened in the past has nothing to do with me! Why can't people just accept I've got a job to do and give me the information I need?'

2 *Head of Corporate Services*: 'I've been with this company since Adam was a boy, long before it became ComTelDat! There have been so many name changes over the years, I sometimes slip and use one of the old names, but then so do many of my colleagues! That's guaranteed to confuse the newcomers! And there are so many of them, sometimes I walk around the floor and don't see a single face I recognise. When I need to know something about a particular area I try to find someone I know working there and ask them. What you don't get with the intranet is the history. Restructuring is a way of life here, but sometimes the new sections/divisions are just the old departments with a different name if you follow my drift. You know that someone, somewhere, is still going to be responsible for – let's say liaison with New Zealand's telecoms industry. But figuring out where they sit in the organisation structure is

just about impossible if you only rely on the intranet. However, if you find the right person, they'll be able to tell you that such and such a section used to be called XYZ – and then bingo! You know where you are. If you're really lucky, you'll find there's another old-timer still in the same role who can let you know the ins and outs of the Australia/NZ business relationship; if you don't get that background you risk making a fool of yourself and damaging the company's reputation. When I started work here it was a government department, lots of rules and bureaucratic mumbo jumbo. It was great to lose all that when the company privatised, I can remember my old boss celebrating when he saw all those filing cabinets and hard-copy files going off to the dump. I'd never admit this to anyone else, but now, just occasionally, I miss those files and the rules we had to follow about writing documents in certain formats, including those special reference numbers at the top of the page. I suppose none of that is necessary with computers now, but at least back in the day you stood a reasonable chance of finding something. The latest thing to land on my lap is leading this team of information specialists, to develop the corporate information governance policy, whatever that may be. Sign of the times I suppose, whereas before we had records managers, file clerks and librarians, now we've got people with all sorts of weird and wonderful titles. Be interesting to find out whether what they do is any different to those file clerks!'

3   *The Business Analyst*: 'I've been really lucky, I joined ComTelDat just last year as a junior analyst and right after I started there was a really big restructuring effort which included the business unit I was assigned to, and staff were offered voluntary redundancies. My manager went, my manager's manager also went, and all of a sudden I was in a really good position as the only person with any knowledge of the ongoing projects that were underway. It's a fantastic opportunity for me, I only completed my uni degree last year and now I've got the chance to put some of the stuff I learned about into practice without any of the old guard being negative about new innovations. To be honest, I might not have lasted under the old management; they weren't exactly encouraging of initiative. I even felt they were a bit put out about how up to date I was, probably scared of being shown up. I really think the people here are trying to make things more difficult than they need to be. They talk about information governance like it's something so big and scary that can't possibly be addressed without an army of consultants providing advice, which is quite frankly ridiculous. They're trying to reinvent the wheel! There's this global industry association that's called the TM

Forum, and they've developed a business process framework called eTOM, which has an accompanying information framework called SID. You can look it up online, but in simple language, eTOM proposes a high-level decomposition of business processes which will work for us, and the SID defines the elements of data which support the business processes. Perhaps I'm missing something, but I really don't see what else we need to do! I mean, this is a global association, so it's really reputable and has to be right for us. I don't believe there's anything different or special about what ComTelDat does, so why don't we just pick this up and apply it? People raise half-hearted objections, like saying that it might not fit the Australian context, or the big one that comes up over and over again about having to get buy-in from the divisions if it's going to be effective. To the first objection I always say that if the Australian context isn't right it's no wonder we're not market leaders – the context needs to change! And as for getting buy-in – I just don't understand why top management doesn't just say this is mandatory, everyone has to use it and that's it, end of story.'

4 *External Contractor*: 'I was over the moon when I was selected as a supplier to the Moving Parts Department at ComTelDat, that's five years ago now. I'm a small business, have only got three employees, and thought with ComTelDat as a customer the future would be really bright. Well it hasn't quite worked out the way I expected, and that's putting it mildly! Communication is the pits, I get sent round and round in circles, and I swear I've aged at least ten years trying to navigate through their answering system if I have a query. My strategy now is to try to find a real live person, someone I can ask for by name, and when I do find someone I try really hard to hang onto them; it's the only way not to get crushed by the ComTelDat systems. Let me give you an example. The reason I have to make contact most often is to chase up unpaid invoices. It's true, I do get a lot of work as a sub-contractor, but getting paid for that work is such a headache; one time the impact on my cash flow was so bad I thought it was going to be the end of my business. With all my other customers I collect what's owed to me by simply e-mailing them an invoice. It's really easy for me to chase up when they don't pay; I've developed this very straightforward process which works like a charm. With ComTelDat however you have to do things their way. I can use a computer ok but this fancy online system they have just defeats me. I can't begin to describe how complicated it is; you submit your invoice, and then wait, and wait … until finally you have to start prodding and trying to find out what's going on and when you can expect payment.

ComTelDat wants you to do that follow-up online, but you can spend half a day trying to get somewhere only to end up in the pit of despair. Fair's fair, I do try to follow their processes, but I honestly can't remember a time when I've managed to get anywhere without having to contact a flesh-and-blood person and beg for help. Usually at that stage I hear "sorry about that, you're not the only one in this situation" and then they'll try to run interference and rescue my invoice from whatever black hole it vanished into. Problem is, you find someone helpful and then try to contact them a couple of months later only to find they've been restructured into some other department and you have to start searching all over again. On top of all that, there's one other area that bugs me. When I was selected as a supplier I was required to sign my life away agreeing to their terms and conditions – lots of stuff about confidentiality and privacy which I didn't really read, but I don't think there was anything I didn't know about in that regard. The bit that keeps worrying me though was something about me having to keep records and those records being subject to company audit. Looking on the bright side though, five years in and nobody's ever mentioned records again so I guess I should stop worrying!'

As the class ran across 12 weeks we were able to introduce the workplace characters one by one and have time to use each to highlight the different and contradictory attitudes and behaviours and discuss what the implications might be for information practices. Finally, the case study was used as the basis for the final assignment, which required the development of a report and project plan for the implementation of a recordkeeping system. Students were encouraged to use the interviews as a source of data to support their recommendations and decision making.

Feedback from students was very positive, with many expressing surprise at just how important people were in developing recordkeeping strategies. We hope that by developing such 'real life' case studies we are not only providing a realistic perspective on the challenges of recordkeeping in current environments, but also helping to equip students with the knowledge and skills needed to effectively contribute to achieving recordkeeping objectives in contemporary settings.

Summary and conclusions

This book has used the concept of information culture and the related, more specific concept of recordkeeping culture to explore the 'people issues' that other research had already identified as 'predominant, fundamental and challenging' (McLeod et al., 2011, p.74). Its main objective has been to provide new perspectives and a set of practical tools to assist records professionals in their complex task of managing the written outcomes and means of people's activities. We have tried to avoid the decontextualised and prescriptive approach typical of existing recordkeeping manuals, models and standards. We strongly believe that each recordkeeping situation involves specific, multifaceted problems that resist any univocal identification, and therefore requires in-depth, situated analyses, where nothing should be taken for granted.

The ICF levels and any relevant cultural and social factors are abstractions, simplifications that we have to rely on for purposes of description. Real-world situations are obviously never that neat. All levels and factors are interrelated and each of the issues we have described may occur at the same time, confusedly and often invisibly. Through our explanations, assessment techniques, toolkit components, suggestions, examples and digressions we hope to have contributed to sharpening our readers' antennas and to making them better equipped to identify and tackle any problem situation that they might face. If training sessions and educational programmes address the areas tackled in this book there is an excellent chance that understandings of and sensitivities to recordkeeping cultures will become embedded in practice.

References

Bolton, R. (1986) *People Skills: how to assert yourself, listen to others, and resolve conflicts,* First Touchstone Edition, Simon & Schuster.

Foscarini, F., Jeurgens, C., Lian, Z. and Oliver, G. (2020). Continuities and Discontinuities: Using Historical Information Culture for Insight into the Sustainability of Innovations. In *International Conference on Information,* 847–59, Springer, Cham.

Ketelaar, E. (2006) 'Control through Communication' in a Comparative Perspective, *Archivaria,* **60,** 71–89.

Ketelaar, E. (2020) Archiving People: a social history of Dutch archives, https://archivisticshome.files.wordpress.com/2020/01/ archiving-people_eric-ketelaar_2020_webversion.pdf [accessed 17 March 2020].

McLeod, J., Childs, S. and Hardiman, R. (2010) *AC+erm Project (Accelerating positive change in electronic records management) – Final Project Report,* www.northumbria.ac.uk/static/5007/ceispdf/final.pdf [accessed 13 August 2012].

Oliver, G., Foscarini, F., Sinclair, C., Nicholls, C. and Loriente, L. (2018) Ethnographic sensitivity and current recordkeeping, *Records Management Journal,* **28** (2), 175–86.

Index